W9-BVY-133

Teach Yourself VISUALLY™

Photoshop® Elements 6

Visual

by Mike Wooldridge and
Linda Wooldridge

ANDERSON COUNTY LIBRARY, ANDERSON, S.C.

BICENTENNIAL
1807
WILEY
2007
BICENTENNIAL

Wiley Publishing, Inc.

Teach Yourself VISUALLY™
Photoshop® Elements 6

Published by
Wiley Publishing, Inc.
10475 Crosspoint Boulevard
Indianapolis, IN 46256

Published simultaneously in Canada

Copyright © 2008 by Wiley Publishing, Inc., Indianapolis, Indiana

No part of this publication may be reproduced, stored in a retrieval system or transmitted in any form or by any means, electronic, mechanical, photocopying, recording, scanning or otherwise, except as permitted under Sections 107 or 108 of the 1976 United States Copyright Act, without either the prior written permission of the Publisher, or authorization through payment of the appropriate per-copy fee to the Copyright Clearance Center, 222 Rosewood Drive, Danvers, MA 01923, 978-750-8400, fax 978-646-8600. Requests to the Publisher for permission should be addressed to the Legal Department, Wiley Publishing, Inc., 10475 Crosspoint Blvd., Indianapolis, IN 46256, 317-572-3447, fax 317-572-4355, online: www.wiley.com/go/permissions.

Library of Congress Control Number: 2007940110

ISBN: 978-0-470-17744-0

Manufactured in the United States of America

10 9 8 7 6 5 4 3 2 1

Trademark Acknowledgments

Wiley, the Wiley Publishing logo, Visual, the Visual logo, Teach Yourself VISUALLY, Read Less - Learn More, and related trade dress are trademarks or registered trademarks of John Wiley & Sons, Inc. and/or its affiliates. Adobe and Photoshop are registered trademarks of Adobe Systems Incorporated. All other trademarks are the property of their respective owners. Wiley Publishing, Inc. is not associated with any product or vendor mentioned in this book.

Wiley Publishing, Inc.

US Sales

Contact Wiley
at (800) 762-2974 or
fax (317) 572-4002.

LIMIT OF LIABILITY/DISCLAIMER OF WARRANTY: THE PUBLISHER AND THE AUTHOR MAKE NO REPRESENTATIONS OR WARRANTIES WITH RESPECT TO THE ACCURACY OR COMPLETENESS OF THE CONTENTS OF THIS WORK AND SPECIFICALLY DISCLAIM ALL WARRANTIES, INCLUDING WITHOUT LIMITATION WARRANTIES OF FITNESS FOR A PARTICULAR PURPOSE. NO WARRANTY MAY BE CREATED OR EXTENDED BY SALES OR PROMOTIONAL MATERIALS. THE ADVICE AND STRATEGIES CONTAINED HEREIN MAY NOT BE SUITABLE FOR EVERY SITUATION. THIS WORK IS SOLD WITH THE UNDERSTANDING THAT THE PUBLISHER IS NOT ENGAGED IN RENDERING LEGAL, ACCOUNTING, OR OTHER PROFESSIONAL SERVICES. IF PROFESSIONAL ASSISTANCE IS REQUIRED, THE SERVICES OF A COMPETENT PROFESSIONAL PERSON SHOULD BE SOUGHT. NEITHER THE PUBLISHER NOR THE AUTHOR SHALL BE LIABLE FOR DAMAGES ARISING HEREFROM. THE FACT THAT AN ORGANIZATION OR WEBSITE IS REFERRED TO IN THIS WORK AS A CITATION AND/OR A POTENTIAL SOURCE OF FURTHER INFORMATION DOES NOT MEAN THAT THE AUTHOR OR THE PUBLISHER ENDORSES THE INFORMATION THE ORGANIZATION OR WEBSITE MAY PROVIDE OR RECOMMENDATIONS IT MAY MAKE. FURTHER, READERS SHOULD BE AWARE THAT INTERNET WEBSITES LISTED IN THIS WORK MAY HAVE CHANGED OR DISAPPEARED BETWEEN WHEN THIS WORK WAS WRITTEN AND WHEN IT IS READ.

FOR PURPOSES OF ILLUSTRATING THE CONCEPTS AND TECHNIQUES DESCRIBED IN THIS BOOK, THE AUTHOR HAS CREATED VARIOUS NAMES, COMPANY NAMES, MAILING, E-MAIL AND INTERNET ADDRESSES, PHONE AND FAX NUMBERS AND SIMILAR INFORMATION, ALL OF WHICH ARE FICTITIOUS. ANY RESEMBLANCE OF THESE FICTITIOUS NAMES, ADDRESSES, PHONE AND FAX NUMBERS AND SIMILAR INFORMATION TO ANY ACTUAL PERSON, COMPANY AND/OR ORGANIZATION IS UNINTENTIONAL AND PURELY COINCIDENTAL.

Contact Us

For general information on our other products and services, please contact our Customer Care Department within the U.S. at 800-762-2974, outside the U.S. at 317-572-3993, or fax 317-572-4002.

For technical support please visit www.wiley.com/techsupport.

Permissions

Brad Herman

www.flickr.com/photos/24thcentury

Brianna Stuart

www.stuartphotography.net

Praise for Visual Books

"Like a lot of other people, I understand things best when I see them visually. Your books really make learning easy and life more fun."

John T. Frey (Cadillac, MI)

"I have quite a few of your Visual books and have been very pleased with all of them. I love the way the lessons are presented!"

Mary Jane Newman (Yorba Linda, CA)

"I just purchased my third Visual book (my first two are dog-eared now!), and, once again, your product has surpassed my expectations.

Tracey Moore (Memphis, TN)

"I am an avid fan of your Visual books. If I need to learn anything, I just buy one of your books and learn the topic in no time. Wonders! I have even trained my friends to give me Visual books as gifts."

Illona Bergstrom (Aventura, FL)

"Thank you for making it so clear. I appreciate it. I will buy many more Visual books."

J.P. Sangdong (North York, Ontario, Canada)

"I have several books from the Visual series and have always found them to be valuable resources."

Stephen P. Miller (Ballston Spa, NY)

"Thank you for the wonderful books you produce. It wasn't until I was an adult that I discovered how I learn – visually. Nothing compares to Visual books. I love the simple layout. I can just grab a book and use it at my computer, lesson by lesson. And I understand the material! You really know the way I think and learn. Thanks so much!"

Stacey Han (Avondale, AZ)

"I absolutely admire your company's work. Your books are terrific. The format is perfect, especially for visual learners like me. Keep them coming!"

Frederick A. Taylor, Jr. (New Port Richey, FL)

"I have several of your Visual books and they are the best I have ever used."

Stanley Clark (Crawfordville, FL)

"I bought my first Teach Yourself VISUALLY book last month. Wow. Now I want to learn everything in this easy format!"

Tom Vial (New York, NY)

"Thank you, thank you, thank you...for making it so easy for me to break into this high-tech world. I now own four of your books. I recommend them to anyone who is a beginner like myself."

Gay O'Donnell (Calgary, Alberta, Canada)

"I write to extend my thanks and appreciation for your books. They are clear, easy to follow, and straight to the point. Keep up the good work! I bought several of your books and they are just right! No regrets! I will always buy your books because they are the best."

Seward Kollie (Dakar, Senegal)

"Compliments to the chef!! Your books are extraordinary! Or, simply put, extra-ordinary, meaning way above the rest! THANK YOU THANK YOU THANK YOU! I buy them for friends, family, and colleagues."

Christine J. Manfrin (Castle Rock, CO)

"What fantastic teaching books you have produced! Congratulations to you and your staff. You deserve the Nobel Prize in Education in the Software category. Thanks for helping me understand computers."

Bruno Tonon (Melbourne, Australia)

"Over time, I have bought a number of your 'Read Less - Learn More' books. For me, they are THE way to learn anything easily. I learn easiest using your method of teaching."

José A. Mazón (Cuba, NY)

"I am an avid purchaser and reader of the Visual series, and they are the greatest computer books I've seen. The Visual books are perfect for people like myself who enjoy the computer, but want to know how to use it more efficiently. Your books have definitely given me a greater understanding of my computer, and have taught me to use it more effectively. Thank you very much for the hard work, effort, and dedication that you put into this series."

Alex Diaz (Las Vegas, NV)

Credits

Project Editor
Sarah Hellert

Acquisitions Editor
Jody Lefevere

Copy Editor
Scott Tullis

Technical Editor
Dennis Cohen

Editorial Manager
Robyn Siesky

Editorial Assistant
Laura Sinise

Business Manager
Amy Knies

Sr. Marketing Manager
Sandy Smith

Manufacturing
Allan Conley
Linda Cook
Paul Gilchrist
Jennifer Guynn

Book Design
Kathie Rickard

Production Coordinator
Erin Smith

Layout
Carrie A. Cesavice
Andrea Hornberger
Jennifer Mayberry

Screen Artist
Joyce Haughey
Jill A. Proll

Illustrators
Ronda David-Burroughs
Cheryl Grubbs

Proofreader
Christine Sabooni

Quality Control
John Greenough

Indexer
Sherry Massey

Wiley Bicentennial Logo
Richard J. Pacifico

Special Help
Barbara Moore

Vice President and Executive Group Publisher
Richard Swadley

Vice President and Publisher
Barry Pruett

Composition Director
Debbie Stailey

About the Authors

Mike Wooldridge is a user-interface designer and inventor. This is his sixth book on Photoshop Elements and his nineteenth in the Visual series.

Linda Wooldridge is a former senior editor at *Macworld*. This is her fifth book in the Visual series.

Authors' Acknowledgments

Mike and Linda thank Sarah Hellert for her top-notch project editing, Dennis Cohen for his knowledgable technical editing, and Scott Tullis for his careful copyediting. It was great working with everyone again! They thank photographers Brad Herman and Brianna Bradley for the use of their beautiful photos in the examples. They also thank their eight-year-old son, who is always is a neverending source of creative ideas, photo-related and otherwise. This book is dedicated to him.

Table of Contents

chapter 3   Organizing Your Photos

chapter 4   Image Editing Basics

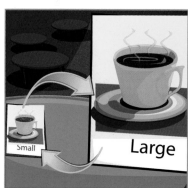

Table of Contents

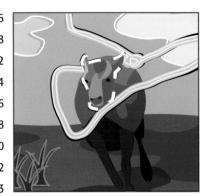

chapter 5 Selection Techniques

chapter 6 Manipulating Selections

chapter 7 Layer Basics

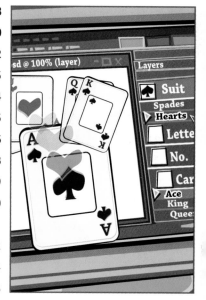

chapter 8 Retouching Photos

Table of Contents

chapter 11 Painting and Drawing on Photos

chapter 12 Applying Filters

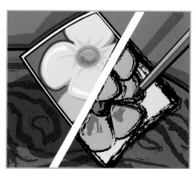

Table of Contents

CHAPTER 1

Getting Started

Are you interested in working with photos on your computer? This chapter introduces you to Adobe Photoshop Elements 6, a popular software application for editing and creating digital images.

Photoshop Elements is a popular photo-editing program you can use to modify, optimize, and organize digital images. You can use the program's Editor to make imperfect snapshots clearer and more colorful, as well as retouch and restore older photos. You can also use the program's Organizer to group your photos into albums, assign descriptive keyword tags, and create slide shows, online galleries, and more.

Manipulate Photos

As its name suggests, Photoshop Elements excels at letting you edit elements in your digital photographs. The program includes numerous image-editing tools and commands you can apply to manipulate the look of your photos. Whether you import photos from a digital camera or a scanner, you can apply a wide variety of editing techniques to your images, from subtle adjustments in color to elaborate filters that make your snapshots look like paintings. See Chapter 6 for more on manipulating selected parts of your photos. See Chapter 11 for more on painting and drawing and Chapter 12 for more on adding effects.

Retouch and Repair

You can use Photoshop Elements to edit new photos as well as retouch and repair older photos that suffer from aging problems. For example, you can restore a faded photo to make it more vibrant, or you can use the Clone Stamp tool to repair a tear or stain. You can also use the program's tools to fix exposure and lighting problems as well as edit out unwanted objects. See Chapter 8 for more on retouching your photos.

Add Elements

Photoshop Elements' painting tools make it a formidable illustration tool as well as photo editor. You can apply colors or patterns to your images with a variety of brush styles. See Chapter 11 to discover how to paint and draw on your photos. In addition, you can use the application's typographic tools to integrate stylized letters and words into your images. See Chapter 13 for more about adding text elements.

Create a Digital Collage

You can combine parts of different images in Photoshop Elements to create a collage. Your compositions can include photos, scanned art, text, and anything else you can save on your computer as a digital image. By placing elements onto separate layers, you can move, transform, and customize them independently of one another. See Chapter 7 for more about layers.

Organize and Catalog

As you bring photos into Photoshop Elements, the program keeps track of them in the Organizer. In the Organizer, you can place groups of photos into theme-specific albums, tag your photos with keywords that describe where they were taken or who is in them, and search for specific photos based on a variety of criteria. See Chapter 3 to read more about the Organizer.

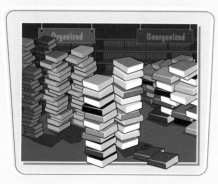

Put Your Photos to Work

After you edit your photographs, you can use them in a variety of ways. Photoshop Elements lets you print your images, save them for the Web, or bring them together into a slide show. You can e-mail your photos to someone else with the Photo Mail feature. You can also create greeting cards, calendars, and other projects. For more on creating and printing your photo projects, see Chapters 15 and 16.

Understanding Digital Images

To work with photos in Photoshop Elements, you must first turn them into a digital format. This section introduces you to some important basics about how computers store images in digital form.

Acquire Photos

You can acquire photographic images to use in Photoshop Elements from a number of sources. You can download photos to Elements from a digital camera or a photo CD. You can scan photographs, slides, or artwork and import the images directly into the program. In addition, you can acquire still images, or *frames*, from digital video. For more on importing photos, see Chapter 2.

Understanding Pixels

Digital images that you download from a camera consist of tiny, solid-color squares called *pixels*. Photoshop Elements works its magic by rearranging and recoloring these squares. You can edit specific pixels or groups of pixels by selecting the area of the photo you want to edit. If you zoom in close, you can see the pixels that make up your image.

Bitmap Images

Images that are composed of pixels are known as *bitmap images*, or sometimes *raster images*. The pixels are arranged in a rectangular grid, and each pixel includes information about its color and position. Most of the time when you are working in Elements you are working with bitmap content.

Vector Graphics

The other common way of displaying pictures on your computer is with vector graphics. Vector graphics encode image information using mathematical equations rather than pixels. Unlike raster images, vector graphics can change size without a loss of quality. When you add shapes or text to your photos in Elements, you are working with vector graphics.

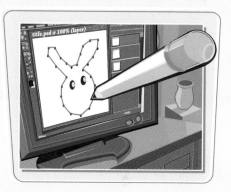

Supported File Formats

Photoshop Elements supports a variety of file types you can both import and export. Popular file formats include BMP, PICT, TIFF, EPS, JPEG, GIF, PNG, and PSD, which stands for Photoshop Document. Files that you save in the PSD format can be shared with other Adobe programs, such as Photoshop and Illustrator. For images that are published on the Internet, JPEG, GIF, and PNG are the most common formats.

File Size

An important way file formats differ from one another is in the amount of storage they take up on your computer. File formats such as PSD and TIFF tend to take up more space because they faithfully save all the information that was originally captured by your camera or other device. Those formats can also include multiple layers. JPEG, GIF, and PNG files, on the other hand, are built to be sent over the Internet and usually sacrifice some quality for the sake of compactness.

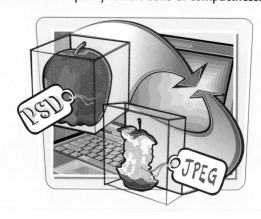

Start Photoshop Elements

You can start Photoshop
Elements and begin creating
and editing digital images.

① Click the **Start** button.

② Type **Elements** in the search box.

Windows displays a list of search results.

③ Click **Adobe Photoshop Elements 6**.

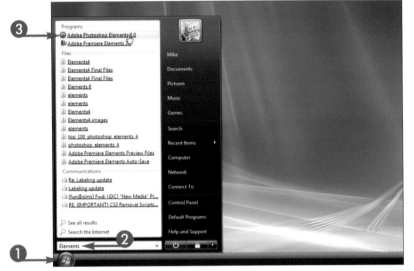

The Photoshop Elements Welcome Screen
opens.

The Welcome Screen displays clickable
icons that take you to different views in
Photoshop Elements.

④ Click **Edit**.

The Photoshop Elements Editor opens.

You can click **Organize**, **Create**, or **Share**
to open the Organizer.

● To change how Elements starts, click here
and choose an option.

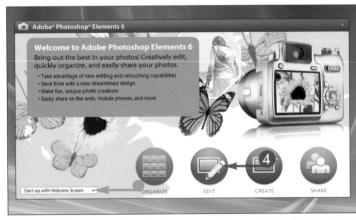

In the Photoshop Elements Editor, you can use a combination of tools, menu commands, and palette-based features to open and edit your digital photos. The main Editor pane displays the photos that you are currently modifying. This section gives you a preview of the interface elements in the Editor.

To open the Editor, click Edit in the Welcome Screen.

Image Window

Displays each photo you open in Photoshop Elements.

Project Bin

Enables you to open and work with multiple photos.

Toolbox

Displays a variety of icons, each representing an image-editing tool.

Options Bar

Displays controls that let you customize the selected tool in the toolbox.

Organizer Button

Clickable button for switching to the Organizer interface, where you can catalog your photos.

Palette Bin

A storage area for frequently used palettes.

Edit Mode Buttons

Clickable buttons for switching between the different editing modes.

Task Tabs

Clickable tabs for switching between workflows in the Editor.

The Organizer Workspace

In the Photoshop Elements Organizer, you can catalog, view, and sort your growing library of digital photos. The main Organizer pane shows miniature versions of the photos in your catalog. This section gives you a preview of the interface elements in the Organizer.

To open the Organizer, click Organize, Create, or Share in the Welcome Screen.

Photo Browser

Displays miniature versions, or *thumbnails*, of the photos in your catalog.

Toolbar

Displays buttons and other options for modifying and sorting photos in the Photo Browser.

Tag Icon

Shows which tags have been applied to a photo.

Display Menu

Contains commands for switching to different views in the Organizer.

Editor Menu

Contains commands for switching to different views in the Editor.

Task Tabs

Clickable tabs for switching between workflows in the Organizer.

Status Bar

Displays the name of the currently open catalog, how many photos are in the catalog, and other summary information.

Palette Bin

A storage area for frequently used palettes.

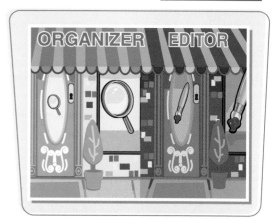

Photoshop Elements has two main views: the Editor and the Organizer. The Editor enables you to modify, combine, and optimize your photos, and the Organizer lets you browse, sort, and categorize photos in your collection. You can easily switch between the two views.

Switch Between the Editor and the Organizer

① Start Photoshop Elements in the Editor view.

Note: *See the section "Start Photoshop Elements" for details on starting the program.*

② Click **Organizer**.

The Organizer appears.

● You can click **Editor** and then **Full Edit** to return to the Editor.

● A lock icon (🔒) appears on any Organizer photos that are currently being edited in the Editor.

To aid in manipulating photos, Photoshop Elements offers a variety of specialized tools that let you edit your image. Take some time to familiarize yourself with the toolbox tools.

Move

Lets you move selected areas of an image.

Zoom

Lets you zoom your view of an image in or out.

Hand

Lets you view unseen parts of larger images.

Eyedropper

Lets you sample color from an area of an image.

Marquee

Lets you select pixels by drawing a box or circle around the area you want to edit.

Lasso

Lets you select pixels by drawing a free-form shape around the area you want to edit.

Magic Wand

Lets you select pixels of odd-shaped areas based on similar pixel color.

Quick Selection Brush

Lets you select pixels using brush shapes.

Straighten

Lets you straighten tilted images.

Cookie Cutter

Lets you crop your image into shapes.

Crop

Lets you trim an image to create a new size.

Type

Lets you add letters and other symbols to an image.

Red-Eye Removal
Lets you correct
red-eye problems.

Spot Healing Brush
Lets you quickly fix slight imperfections
by cloning nearby pixels.

Clone Stamp
Lets you duplicate an
area of the image.

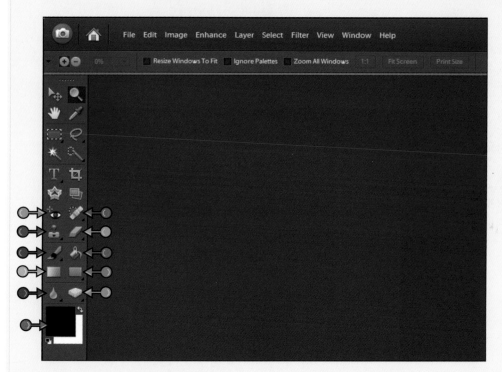

Eraser
Lets you erase pixels.

Brush
Lets you paint strokes
of color.

Paint Bucket
Lets you fill areas with
color.

Gradient
Lets you create
blended color effects
to use as fills.

Custom Shape
Lets you draw
predefined shapes.

Foreground and Background Colors
Lets you set the foreground and
background colors that different tools apply.

Sponge
Lets you adjust color
saturation or intensity.

Blur
Lets you blur objects
in your image.

Work with Toolbox Tools

You can use the tools in Photoshop Elements' toolbox to make changes to an image. Positioning the mouse pointer over a tool displays the tool name. After you click to select a tool, the Options bar displays controls for customizing how the tool works. Some tools have a tiny triangle in the corner indicating hidden tools you can select. For example, the Marquee tool has two variations: Rectangular and Elliptical.

Work with Toolbox Tools

SELECT A TOOL

1 Position the mouse pointer (⟨⟩) over a tool.

● A label appears displaying the tool name. You can click the tool name to access Help information about the tool.

2 Click a tool to select it.

The Options bar displays customizing options for the selected tool.

3 Specify any options you want for the tool.

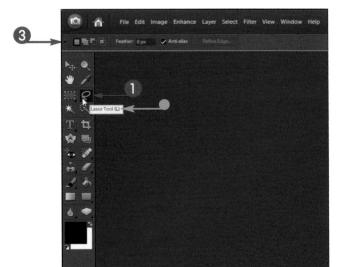

SELECT A HIDDEN TOOL

1 Click a tool that has a triangle in its corner.

2 Press and hold the mouse button.

A menu of hidden tools appears.

3 Click the tool you want to use.

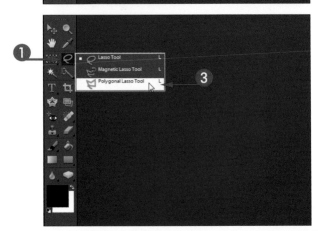

MOVE THE TOOLBOX

1 Position the mouse pointer (⬉) over the top of the docked toolbox.

2 Drag the toolbox to a new location on the screen.

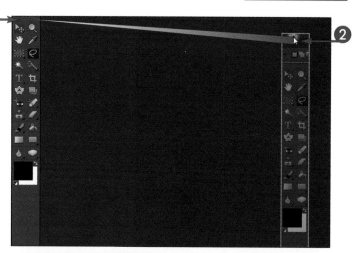

3 Release the mouse button.

● Photoshop Elements displays the toolbox as a floating palette.

You can drag the toolbox to another location by dragging the top of the palette.

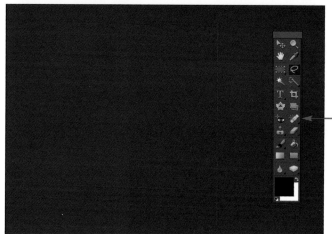

TIPS

How do I close the floating toolbox?

Closing the toolbox palette closes the toolbox entirely so that the tools no longer appear on-screen. To close the floating toolbox palette, click **Window**, and then click **Tools**. To reopen the palette, click **Window** and then **Tools** again. If the toolbox is floating, you can press Tab to open or close it.

How do I dock my floating toolbox again?

Position the mouse pointer (⬉) over the top of the toolbox palette, and then click and drag the toolbox to the left side of the program window. Photoshop Elements automatically docks it for you when you drag it close enough to the left edge of the window.

You can open free-floating windows called *palettes* to access different Photoshop Elements commands and features. You can store the palettes you use the most in the Palette Bin for easy access. You can collapse and expand palettes in the Palette Bin.

For more on the location of the Palette Bin, see the section "The Editor Workspace."

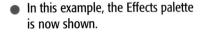

EXPAND OR COLLAPSE A PALETTE IN THE PALETTE BIN

① Click the triangle next to the palette name in the Palette Bin.

● Click the **Expand** arrow (▶) to display a collapsed palette.

● Click the **Collapse** arrow (▼) to collapse a palette from view.

● In this example, the Effects palette is now shown.

OPEN A NEW PALETTE

① Click **Window**.

② Click the palette name.

A check mark () next to the palette name indicates the palette is already open.

● The palette opens.

You can move the palette by dragging its title bar.

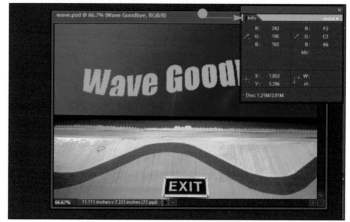

TIPS

How do I add a palette to the Palette Bin?

Open the palette as a free-floating window and then click the palette menu's **More** button. This displays a menu of related palette commands. Next, click **Place in Palette Bin when Closed**. After you close the palette, Photoshop Elements adds the palette to the Palette Bin.

How do I minimize a free-floating palette?

Double-click the palette's title to minimize the palette window. To view the full palette again, double-click the title.

continued

You can move palettes around the program window to suit the way you work. You can close a palette you no longer want to view. You can also hide the Palette Bin to free up more on-screen workspace.

Work with Palettes *(continued)*

MOVE A PALETTE

1. Click and drag the palette title to the work area.

2. Release the mouse.

   The palette opens as a free-floating window.

   ● You can click the **More** button to access commands relevant to the palette.

   You can resize the Palette Bin by dragging the bin's border.

CLOSE A PALETTE

1. Click the **Close** button (✖).

   The palette closes.

CLOSE THE PALETTE BIN

1 Click the **Close Palette Bin** button (▶).

You can also click **Window** and then click **Palette Bin**.

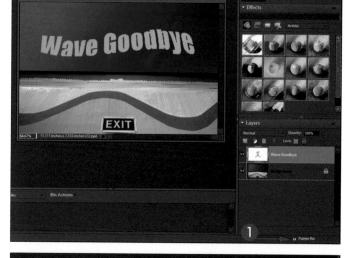

The Palette Bin closes.

● To display the bin again, click the **Open Palette Bin** button (◀).

TIP

Can I customize a palette?

You can customize some of the palettes in Photoshop Elements. For example, you can change the size of the thumbnail image that appears in the Layers palette. To customize a palette, follow these steps:

1 Click here.

2 Click **Palette Options**.

The palette's Options dialog box opens.

3 Make any changes to the palette options.

4 Click **OK**.

Elements applies the changes to the palette.

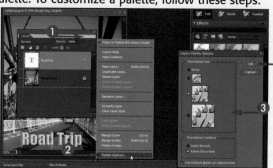

Set Program Preferences

Photoshop Elements' Preferences dialog box lets you change default settings and customize how the program looks. The Preferences dialog box includes nine categories: General, Saving Files, Performance, Display & Cursors, Transparency, Units & Rulers, Grid, Plug-Ins, and Type. You can view and select from different settings in each category.

① Click **Edit**.

② Click **Preferences**.

③ Click **General**.

The Preferences dialog box appears and displays General options.

④ Select any settings you want to change.

● For example, you can specify the shortcut keys for stepping backward and forward through your commands.

⑤ Click a different preference category.

● You can also click **Prev** and **Next** to move back and forth between categories.

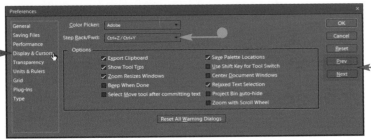

In this example, the Preferences dialog box shows Display & Cursors options.

6 Select any settings you want to change.

● For example, you can specify the shape of the painting tool cursors.

7 Click a different preference category.

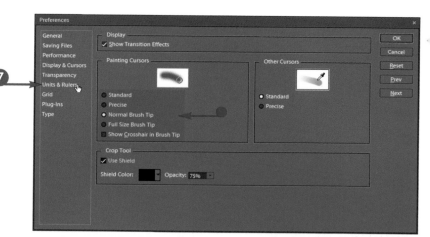

In this example, the Preferences dialog box displays Units & Rulers options.

8 Select any settings you want to change.

● For example, you can specify the default units for various aspects of the program.

9 Click **OK**.

Photoshop Elements sets the preferences to your specifications.

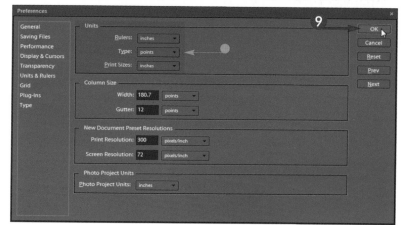

TIPS

What type of measurement units should I use in Elements?

Typically, you should use the units most applicable to the type of output you intend to produce. Pixel units are useful for Web imaging because monitor dimensions are measured in pixels. Inches or picas are useful for print because those are standards for working on paper. You can find measurement settings in the Units & Rulers preferences.

How do I allocate extra memory to Elements for opening more image files?

Digital image-editing programs can use up a lot of random access memory, or *RAM*. The Performance preferences show how much memory you have available and how much of it Photoshop Elements is using. You can make changes to these settings to enhance the program's performance. The Scratch Disks preferences enable you to allocate extra memory on your hard drive, called *scratch disk space*, to use if your computer runs out of RAM.

Photoshop Elements comes with plenty of electronic documentation that you can access whenever you need help.

Find Help

1 Click **Help**.

2 Click **Photoshop Elements Help**.

The Help documentation opens in a Web browser with help topics on the left.

● You can click **Index** to list help topics alphabetically.

3 Click here to view a list of subtopics (+ changes to –).

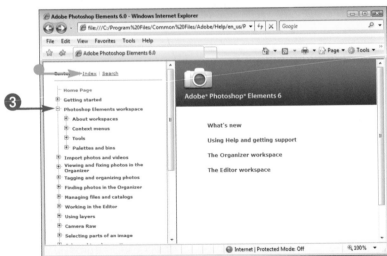

A list of subtopics appears.

④ Click the topic you want to view.

● The Help system displays information about the topic in the right-hand frame.

You can scroll through the information and click links to learn more about a topic.

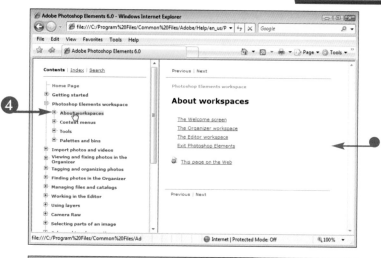

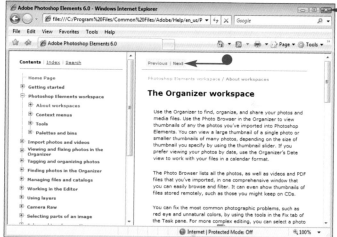

● You can click **Previous** and **Next** to move between topics.

⑤ Click the **Close** button ( ).

The Help documentation browser window closes.

TIPS

How do I search for a particular topic?
You can use the search feature in the Help documentation to look up keywords. Click **Search** in the top-left corner, type your search keywords in the text box, and then click **Search**. Photoshop Elements displays any matching search results as a list of clickable links.

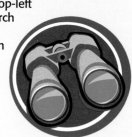

How can I get additional tips and news about Photoshop Elements?
If you have an Internet connection, you can click **Help** and then click **Online Support** to open the Support Web page on the Adobe Web site. Here you can access an up-to-date knowledge base that covers technical issues related to Elements. You can also click **Help** and then click **Online Learning Resources** to access a Web page with links to Elements tutorials and other educational tools.

Getting Digital Photos into Elements

Before you can start working with photos in Photoshop Elements, you must first import them from a camera, scanner, or other digital device, or from folders on your computer. This chapter shows you how to import photos into the Elements Organizer and open them in the Elements Editor.

Get Photos for Your Projects

In order to work with images in Photoshop Elements, you must first acquire the images. You can get raw material for Elements from a variety of sources.

Digital Cameras

A digital camera is probably the most common way to create your digital photos and then get them onto your computer. Most digital cameras save their images as JPEG or TIFF files, both of which you can open and edit in Photoshop Elements. You can transfer images directly from a camera using a USB cable, or you can transfer images using a card reader, a device that reads your camera's memory card.

Scanned Photos and Art

A scanner gives you an inexpensive way to convert existing paper-based content into digital form. You can scan photos and art into your computer, retouch and stylize them in Photoshop Elements, and then output them to a color printer. You can also use a slide attachment to digitize slides using a scanner.

Web Images

If you are interested in photos or art stored on the Web, you can easily save those image files to your computer and then open them in Photoshop Elements. In Microsoft Internet Explorer on the PC, you can save a Web image by right-clicking it and selecting the **Save Picture As** command. There are many inexpensive stock photo Web sites that offer professional-grade content for download. On photo-sharing sites such as Flickr, users often allow noncommercial use of their photos.

Start from Scratch

You can also create your Photoshop Elements image from scratch by opening a blank canvas in the image window. You can then apply colors and patterns with the painting tools or cut and paste parts of other images to create a composite. See the section "Create a Blank Image" for more on opening a blank canvas.

Film Photos

If you have a film camera, you can have your photos burned to a CD during film processing. Then you can import the photos from the CD just as you would import photos from a folder on your computer. See the section "Import Photos from a Folder" for details.

Working with Imported Photos

When you import images into Photoshop Elements, they are stored in the program's Organizer. There you can browse miniature versions of your photos, called *thumbnails*, sort them, group them into albums, and assign keyword tags to them. You can edit your photos by opening them in the Elements Editor. You can open them in the Editor from the Organizer or open them directly from folders on your computer.

Import Photos from a Digital Camera or Card Reader

You can bring photos into Photoshop Elements from a digital camera or directly from the camera's memory card. Most cameras and card readers manufactured today connect to a computer through a USB port. A typical PC comes with multiple USB ports. Make sure the device is hooked up properly before you begin. Also, some computers have special media slots that accept memory cards for transferring photos and other files.

Every camera and card reader works differently, so be sure to consult the documentation that came with your device for more information.

Import Photos from a Digital Camera or Card Reader

① In the Organizer, click **File**.

Note: For details about using the Organizer, see Chapter 3.

② Click **Get Photos and Videos**.

③ Click **From Camera or Card Reader**.

The Photo Downloader window opens.

Photo Downloader may automatically open when you connect your device to your computer, depending on the settings in Elements.

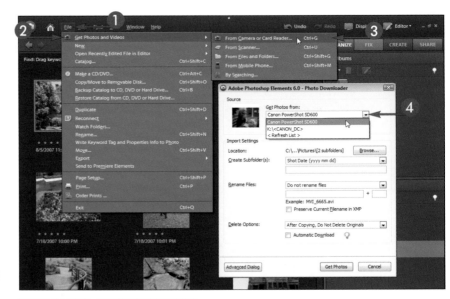

④ Click here and select your camera or memory card.

By default, Elements downloads your photos into dated subfolders inside your Pictures folder.

● You can click **Browse** to select a different download location.

● You can click here to select a different naming scheme for the subfolders.

⑤ Click here and select a naming scheme for your files.

⑥ Click here to select whether to keep your photos on the device or delete them after downloading.

● You can click this option to enable Elements to download your photos automatically using the current settings whenever a photo device is connected to your computer (■ changes to ✓).

⑦ Click **Get Photos**.

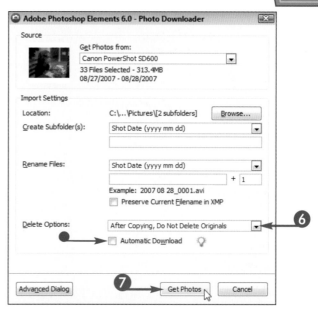

Photoshop Elements downloads the photos from the device.

Elements automatically fixes red-eye by default. See the tip for details on turning this feature off.

After downloading the photos, Elements adds them to the current Organizer catalog. There you can add the photos to albums and perform other functions.

 TIP

What is the Advanced Dialog button in the Photo Downloader?

The Advanced dialog box gives you access to additional import features.

① Click **Advanced Dialog** in the bottom left corner of the Photo Downloader.

The Advanced dialog box opens.

② Click to select each photo you want to import from your device (■ changes to ✓).

③ Click here to turn off red-eye correction, which is on by default (✓ changes to ■).

④ Type author and copyright details to be applied to all the imported photos here.

⑤ Click **Get Photos**.

Import Photos from a Scanner

You can bring a photo into Photoshop Elements through a scanner attached to your computer. You can scan black-and-white and color photos to import into Elements. To scan an image, make sure the scanner is hooked up properly before you begin. Some scanners include slide attachments that enable you to digitize slides as well.

Every scanner works differently, so be sure to consult the documentation that came with your scanner for details.

Import Photos from a Scanner

① In the Organizer, click **File**.

Note: For details about using the Organizer, see Chapter 3.

② Click **Get Photos and Videos**.

③ Click **From Scanner**.

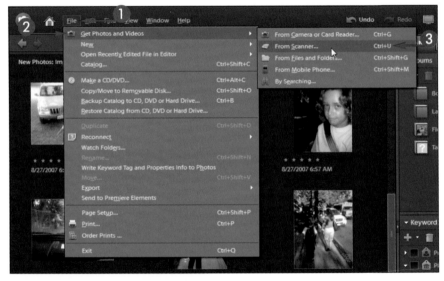

The Get Photos from Scanner window opens.

④ Click here and select your scanner.

By default, Elements saves scanned photos in the Adobe folder inside your Pictures folder.

● You can click **Browse** to select another location.

⑤ Click here to select a file format.

Note: For more about file formats, see Chapter 16.

⑥ Click **OK**.

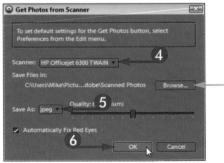

The software associated with your scanner opens.

⑦ Change your scanning settings as needed. You may need to specify whether the photo is black and white or color. You may also get to preview the scan.

⑧ Click a button to scan your photo using the scanner software.

The image is scanned and added to the current catalog in the Organizer.

● Elements displays the imported photo by itself.

⑨ Click **Show All** to view your entire catalog of photos.

How can I adjust the default settings for importing photos?
You can adjust the default settings for importing photos from a scanner or other device in the Preferences dialog box.

① Click **Edit**, **Preferences**, and then **Scanner**.

The Scanner preferences appear.

② Adjust the default settings.

● You can adjust the default settings for getting photos from a camera or card reader by clicking here.

③ Click **OK**.

Photoshop Elements displays those setings the next time you scan a photo.

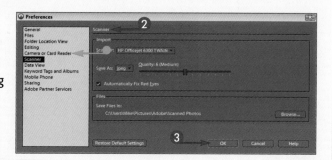

Import Photos from a Folder

You can use Photoshop Elements' Organizer program to import images from a folder on your computer or a disc. You may find this useful if you already have an archive of digital photos on your PC or on photo CDs.

Import Photos from a Folder

① In the Organizer, click **File**.

Note: For details about using the Organizer, see Chapter 3.

② Click **Get Photos and Videos**.

③ Click **From Files and Folders**.

The Get Photos from Files and Folders window appears.

④ Click here and select the folder containing your photos.

⑤ Ctrl-click to select the photos you want to import. You can press Ctrl + A to select all of the photos in the folder.

● Elements automatically fixes red-eye by default. You can click to skip this step (✓ changes to ■).

● You can import different types of files, such as PDF documents or Photoshop Elements projects, by clicking here.

6 Click **Get Photos**.

Photoshop Elements downloads the selected photos from the folder.

Elements displays the imported photos by themselves in the Organizer.

7 Click **Show All** to view your entire catalog of photos.

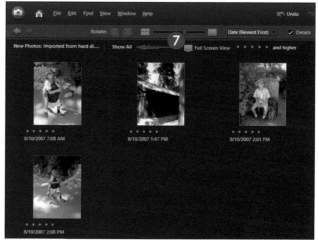

TIP

How can I quickly search my entire computer for photos to import?

Photoshop Elements has a search feature that scans your hard disks for folders that contain digital photos. You can then import the photos from those folders all at once.

1 Click **File**, **Get Photos and Videos**, and then **By Searching**.

2 In the search dialog box, click here and select all hard disks, a single hard disk, or a folder.

3 Click **Search**.

● Elements performs a search and displays a list of photo-containing folders.

4 Select one or more folders and then click **Import Folders** to get the photos.

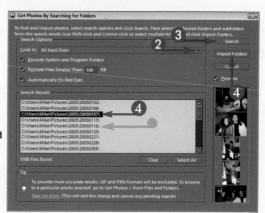

Watch a Folder for New Images

Photoshop Elements can watch certain folders on your computer for the addition of new photos. You can have Elements notify you when it recognizes new photos or have it import those photos automatically. The imported photos are added to your Organizer catalog.

Watch a Folder for New Images

① In the Organizer, click **File**.

Note: *For details about using the Organizer, see Chapter 3.*

② Click **Watch Folders**.

The Watch Folders window appears.

● By default, Photoshop Elements is configured to watch your Pictures folder.

③ Click **Add**.

The Browse For Folder dialog box appears.

④ Select a folder to watch.

⑤ Click **OK**.

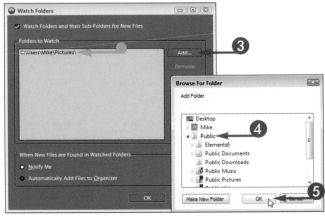

The folder appears in the watch list.

● You can click here to watch subfolders inside your watched folders (■ changes to ✓).

● You can select whether to receive alerts about new images or to have Elements add photos to the Organizer automatically (● changes to ○).

6 Click **OK**.

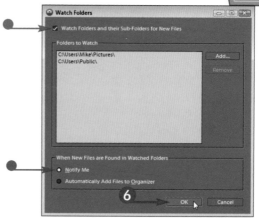

RECEIVE A WATCH NOTIFICATION

1 Exit Photoshop Elements and then add new photos to a watched folder on your computer.

To get new photos, see some of the other tasks in this chapter.

2 Start Photoshop Elements and open the Organizer.

● Photoshop Elements alerts you to the new photos in your watched folders.

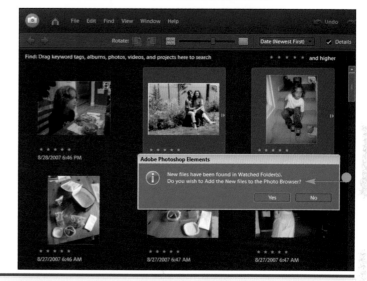

TIP

How can I make Photoshop Elements automatically download photos when I connect my camera?

1 Click **Edit**, **Preferences**, and then **Camera or Card Reader**.

The Camera or Card Reader Preferences open.

2 Click to select the **Auto Launch** option (■ changes to ✓).

3 Click **Edit**.

4 In the Edit Download Option dialog box, click here and then click **Automatic Download**.

5 Click **OK**.

6 Click **OK** in the Preferences dialog box.

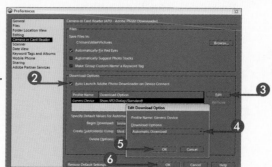

You can open a photo in the Photoshop Elements Editor to modify it or use it in a project. You can also open photos from the Organizer for editing in the Editor.

Open a Photo

OPEN A PHOTO FROM A FOLDER

① In the Editor, click **File**.

Note: For details about opening the Editor, see Chapter 1.

② Click **Open**.

The Open dialog box appears.

③ Navigate to the folder containing the file you want to open.

④ Click the photo you want to open.

● A preview of the image appears.

⑤ Click **Open**.

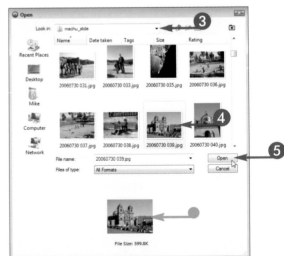

Photoshop Elements opens the image.

- The file name and zoom value appear in the title bar.

- If the Photo Bin is open in the Editor, the image also appears in the bin.

- If you open multiple photos at once, you can click **Window** to view a list of the open photos.

OPEN AN ORGANIZER PHOTO FOR EDITING

1 In the Organizer, right-click the photo you want to edit.

Note: For details about using the Organizer, see Chapter 3.

2 In the menu that appears, click **Full Edit**.

Photoshop Elements opens the photo in the Editor.

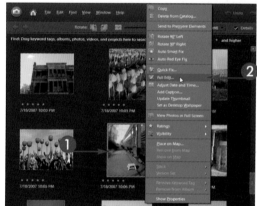

What types of files can Photoshop Elements open? Photoshop Elements can open most of the image file formats in common use today. Here are a few of the more popular ones:	BMP (Bitmap)	The standard Windows image format
	TIFF (Tagged Image File Format)	A popular format for print
	EPS (Encapsulated PostScript)	Another print-oriented format
	JPEG (Joint Photographic Experts Group)	A format for Web images
	GIF (Graphics Interchange Format)	Another format for Web images
	PNG (Portable Network Graphics)	Yet another format for Web images
	PSD (Photoshop Document)	Photoshop's native file format

You can start a Photoshop Elements project by creating a blank image, and then you can add photographic, text, and other content to the blank image.

You can add content from other images as separate layers. For more about layers, see Chapter 7.

Create a Blank Image

1 In the Editor, click **File**.

Note: For details about opening the Editor, see Chapter 1.

2 Click **New**.

3 Click **Blank File**.

The New dialog box appears.

4 Type a name for the new image.

5 Type the desired dimensions and resolution, or click to select a preset dimension and resolution.

● You can click here to change the background of the blank canvas.

6 Click **OK**.

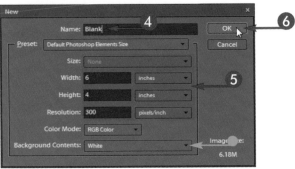

Photoshop Elements creates a new image window at the specified dimensions.

⑦ Use the Photoshop Elements tools and commands to edit the new image.

● In this example, parts of other photos were cut and pasted onto the blank image.

● The parts appear in different layers in the Layers palette.

Note: See Chapter 7 for more about layers.

Note: To save your image, see the section "Save a Photo."

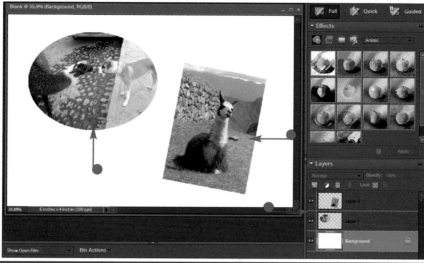

What should I choose as a resolution for a new image?

The appropriate resolution depends on how you will eventually use the image. For Web or multimedia images, select 72 pixels/inch — the standard resolution for on-screen images. If you are printing black-and-white images on regular paper using a laser printer, 150 pixels/inch will probably suffice. For full-color magazine or brochure images, you should use a higher resolution — at least 250 pixels/inch.

How do I open a frame from a video clip?

You can open a video frame in Photoshop Elements by clicking **File**, **Import**, and then **Frame from Video**. A dialog box appears that enables you to browse for and open a video clip, scan through the clip, and then import a frame into the Elements Editor. You can then edit the frame as you would any other photo. Elements lets you import from WMV, MPEG, and AVI video files, but not from MOV files.

Save a Photo

You can save a photo in Photoshop Elements to store any changes that you made to it. PSD is the default file format for Elements. Elements supports a variety of other image file formats, including the popular JPEG, GIF, and PNG formats commonly found on the Web.

New in Elements 6, you can have multiple versions of the same image saved as a version set in the Organizer.

Save a Photo

① In the Editor, click **File**.

Note: For details about opening the Editor, see Chapter 1.

② Click **Save As**.

*Note: For photos that you have previously saved, you can click **File** and then **Save**.*

The Save As dialog box appears.

③ Type a name for the file.

● You can click here and select another folder or drive in which to store the file.

● You can click here to select another file format.

Note: See Chapter 16 for more about file formats.

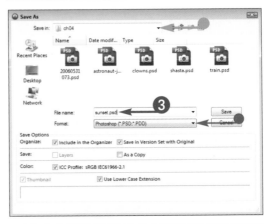

④ Click to select the option to include the saved file in the Organizer (■ changes to ✓).

⑤ Click to select the option to save the edited file with other versions of the same file in the Organizer (■ changes to ✓).

You can save a photo into a version set only when the photo already exists as a version in the Organizer.

⑥ Click **Save**.

Photoshop Elements saves the image file.

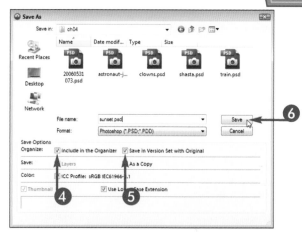

VIEW A VERSION SET IN THE ORGANIZER

① In the Organizer, find a version set. Version sets have light gray boxes around them and are marked with a version icon (▣).

Note: For details about using the Organizer, see Chapter 3.

● You can use the scroll bar to browse your photos.

② Click to expand (▣) the version set so you can view all the photos in that set.

Photoshop Elements expands the version set.

In the Editor, how can I save all of my open photos as an album in the Organizer?

① In the Editor, open the photos you want to save as an album.

② In the Photo Bin, click **Bin Actions**.

③ Click **Save Bin as an Album**.

④ Type a name for the album.

⑤ Click **OK**.

The photos are saved as a new album in the Organizer.

Note: For more about albums, see Chapter 3.

Duplicate a Photo

In the Editor, you can duplicate a photo to keep an unchanged copy while you continue to work on the duplicate. Photoshop Elements puts the duplicate in its own window.

Duplicate a Photo

1 In the Editor, click **File**.

Note: For details about opening the Editor, see Chapter 1.

2 Click **Duplicate**.

The Duplicate Image dialog box opens.

● Photoshop Elements displays an editable name for the duplicate.

3 Click **OK**.

● Photoshop Elements opens a duplicate of the photo in a new window.

● The name and zoom value appear in the title bar.

Note: See the section "Save a Photo" for details on how to save the duplicate.

You can close a photo after you finish editing it. Although you can have more than one photo open at a time, closing photos you no longer need can speed up your computer's performance.

Close a Photo

① In the Editor, click **File**.

Note: *For details about opening the Editor, see Chapter 1.*

② Click **Close**.

● You can also click here to close a photo.

● If you have not saved the file, Elements prompts you to do so before closing the file. Click **Yes** to save your work.

Note: *See the section "Save a Photo" for more on how to save files.*

After saving, if needed, Photoshop Elements closes the photo. The program remains open.

Organizing Your Photos

Are you ready to organize your digital photos? You can catalog, view, and sort photo files using the Organizer. A complement to the Editor in Photoshop Elements, the Organizer helps you manage your growing library of digital pictures by categorizing them in a variety of ways. This chapter shows you how to take advantage of the Organizer's many photo-management features.

Introducing the Organizer

You can use the Organizer program to manage your growing library of digital photos. As you open or import photos into Photoshop Elements, they are automatically added to the Organizer catalog. In the Organizer, you can sort and filter your photo collection in different ways. You can also group photos into albums, tag them with descriptive keywords, and even place them on a geographic map.

Virtual Browser

The Organizer acts as a virtual browser, enabling you to view *thumbnails,* or miniature versions of your pictures. The thumbnails you see in the Organizer are merely "pointers" to the original file location. The images remain intact in their original location unless you decide to delete them. The Organizer enables you to view your photos from one convenient window. See the sections "View Photos in the Photo Browser" and "View Photos by Date" to learn more.

Catalog

When you bring photo files into the Organizer, the program adds them to your catalog of images. Images are cataloged by date. You can keep all of your photos in one catalog, or you can store them in separate catalogs. If you want to group your photos further, you can place them into albums or stacks. See the sections "Create a Catalog," "Work with Albums," and "Stack Photos" to learn more.

Keyword Tags

You can use keyword tags to help you sort and track your photos. A *keyword tag* is a text identifier you assign to a photo. After you assign tags, you can then sort through your catalog for pictures matching a certain tag. You can assign any of the preset tags that come with the Organizer, or you can create your own. The Organizer's presets include tags for people, family, friends, places, and more. You can also assign multiple tags to the same photo. See the section "Work with Keyword Tags" to learn more.

Map Photos

Have you ever wanted to pull up photos that were taken in a particular location, such as a favorite vacation spot or where you used to live? The Organizer helps you associate your photos with certain places by letting you put them on a geographic map. Once you have mapped your photos, they appear as red pins on the map. You can navigate your collection by scrolling and zooming to different countries, cities, and streets.

Find Photos

As your photo collection grows, being able to find photos efficiently becomes critically important. Although filtering photos by album or keyword tag offers one way to find photos, the Organizer also includes full-featured searching tools. You can search your catalog by date, file name, caption, camera model, map location, and more. You can even mix multiple search criteria to create more powerful searches. See the section "Find Photos" for more information.

Creations

Because it lets you easily organize and find photos in your collection, the Organizer is an important first step in completing various Photoshop Elements projects. For example, you can display your favorite photos in the Organizer and then create a custom slide show to distribute to friends and family. You can also create online photo galleries, greeting cards, postage stamps, and more. See Chapter 15 for photo projects you can build in Elements.

You can organize and manage your digital photos in Elements' Organizer. The Organizer works alongside Elements' Editor to help you keep track of the digital photos and other media you store on your computer. You can open the Organizer from the Welcome screen that appears when you start up Photoshop Elements or switch to it from the Editor.

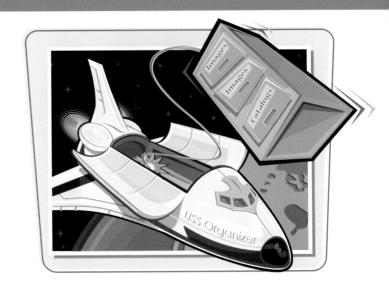

Open the Organizer

FROM THE WELCOME WINDOW

① Start Photoshop Elements.

Note: See Chapter 1 for more about starting Elements.

The Welcome Screen appears.

② Click **Organize** to open the Organizer.

● You can click **Create** to open the Organizer in the Create view.

● You can click **Share** to open the Organizer in the Share view.

The Organizer opens.

Note: To import photos into the Organizer workspace, see Chapter 2.

Note: To create a new catalog with which to organize your photos, see the section "Create a Catalog" in this chapter.

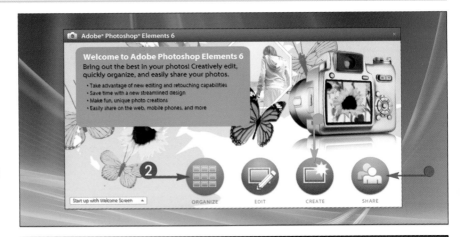

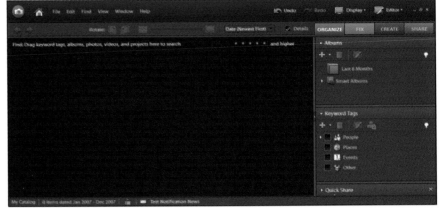

FROM THE EDITOR

1. Start Photoshop Elements.

2. From the Welcome Screen that appears, click **Edit** to open the Editor.

3. Click **Organizer**.

The Organizer opens.

● To return to the Editor, click **Editor** and then select a menu option.

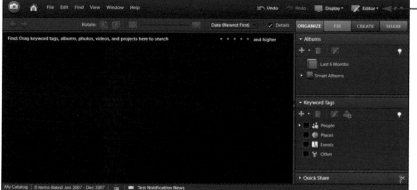

 TIP

Can I tell Photoshop Elements to automatically go to the Organizer at startup?

Yes. You can specify whether you want to view the Welcome Screen, the Editor, or the Organizer when you start the program. To set the Organizer to start automatically, follow these steps:

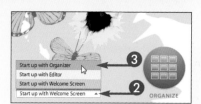

1. Start Photoshop Elements.

2. In the Welcome Screen, click here.

3. Click **Start up with Organizer**.

   The next time you open Photoshop Elements, the Organizer will open automatically.

Create a Catalog

The photos you manage in the Organizer are stored in catalogs. You can keep your photos in one large catalog or separate them into smaller catalogs. When you start the Organizer, Elements creates a default catalog for you called My Catalog.

You can organize your photos within a catalog into smaller groups called albums. See the section "Work with Albums" for details.

Create a Catalog

1. In the Organizer, click **File**.

2. Click **Catalog**.

● You can restore a catalog you have previously backed up by clicking **Restore Catalog from CD, DVD, or Hard Disk**. See Chapter 16 for more about backing up photos.

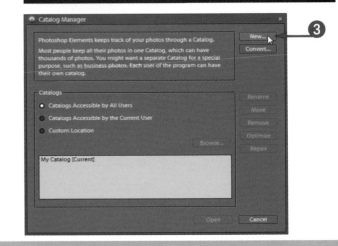

The Catalog Manager dialog box appears.

Elements lists the available catalogs.

3. Click **New**.

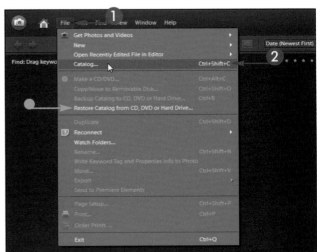

④ Type a name for the new catalog.

⑤ Click **OK**.

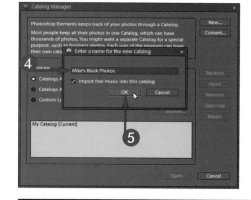

Photoshop Elements creates the new catalog and opens it.

● Elements displays the name of the current catalog and the number of photos it includes.

● The range of dates for the content in the current catalog is here.

Note: *To add photos to your catalog, see Chapter 2.*

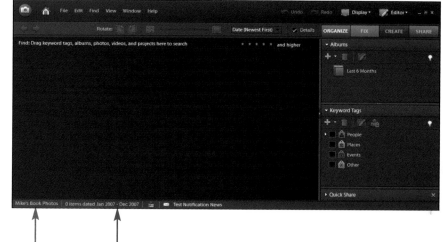

How do I switch to a different catalog in the Organizer?

Open the Catalog Manager by following steps **1** and **2** above. Select the catalog that you want to open in the catalog list and then click **Open**. You can open only one catalog at a time in the Organizer.

How can I protect the photos in the Organizer from viewing by others?

You can edit a catalog so that it is accessible only by the user who is currently logged in on your computer. Open the Catalog Manager by following steps **1** and **2** above. From the list that appears, select the catalog that you want to protect and click **Move**. A dialog box appears, letting you change the accessibility of the catalog.

View Photos in
the Photo Browser

After you add photos to your catalog, you can view them using the Organizer's Photo Browser. The Photo Browser displays thumbnails, or miniature versions of your photos, along with details about those photos. You can filter, sort, and change the size of the thumbnails.

View Photos in the Photo Browser

① Open the Organizer.

The Photo Browser displays the photos in the Organizer catalog.

● Photos are sorted from newest to oldest by default.

② Click and drag the thumbnail slider (▣) to the right.

● The thumbnails enlarge. You can click here to maximize the thumbnails (▣).

Dragging the slider (▣) to the left decreases the size of the thumbnails. You can click to minimize the thumbnails (▦).

● You can use the scrollbar to browse other available thumbnails in the Photo Browser.

③ Click here and click **Date (Oldest First)**.

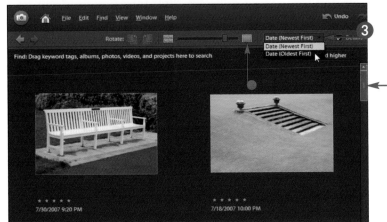

The sorting order reverses in the Photo Browser, with the oldest photos at the top.

④ Click **Display**.

⑤ Click **View Photos in Full Screen**.

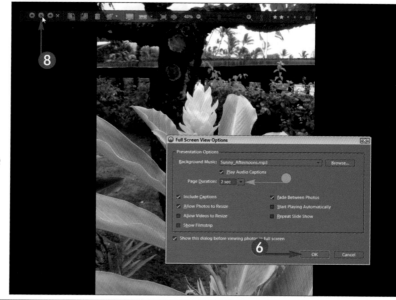

The Photo Browser switches to full-screen view.

● You can select photo duration and other slide show settings in the dialog box.

⑥ Click **OK** to close the dialog box.

⑦ Drag your mouse to the top of the screen.

A navigation bar appears.

⑧ Click the **Play** button (▶) to start the slide show.

You can press Esc to exit full-screen view and return to the Photo Browser.

How can I hide certain file types in the Photo Browser?

The Photo Browser can help you organize not only photos but also video files, audio files, creative projects built in Elements, and PDF files. You can filter the file types that are displayed in the Photo Browser.

① In the Organizer, click **View**.

② Click **Media Types**.

Media types that are shown are checked.

③ Click a checked media type.

Elements hides the media type in the Photo Browser.

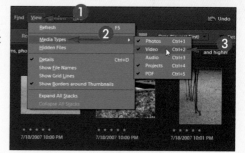

Work with Albums

Albums are a way to organize your photos within an Organizer catalog. For example, you can take photos shot at a particular time or place and group them as an album. This makes it easier to find the photos later.

You can also organize photos in a catalog using tags. See the section "Work with Keyword Tags" in this chapter for details.

Work with Albums

CREATE A NEW ALBUM

1 In the Organizer, open the catalog within which you want to create an album.

2 Open the Albums palette in the Organizer bin.

3 Click plus (➕) and click **New Album**.

The Create Album dialog box opens.

4 Type a name for the album.

● You can assign the album to an album group.

● You can add a descriptive note about the album.

5 Click **OK**.

● The Organizer adds the new album to the Albums palette.

ASSIGN A PHOTO TO AN ALBUM

① Click and drag the photo from the Photo Browser to an album.

The Organizer adds the photo to the album and applies the album's icon.

● You can also click and drag the album, label in the Albums palette and drop it onto the photo in the Organizer.

To add multiple images to an album, press and hold Ctrl while clicking photos and then drag the photos as a group to the Albums palette.

VIEW AN ALBUM

① Click the album name in the Albums palette.

● A show icon (▦) appears next to the album name.

The Organizer displays all the photos in the album.

Photos assigned to an album are marked with an Album icon (▣).

● You can click **Show All** to return to the entire catalog.

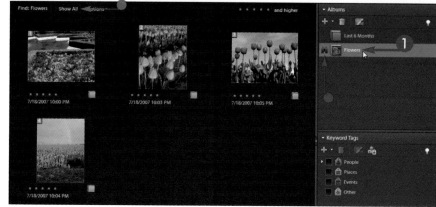

How do I remove an album?

Removing an album does not remove the images from the Organizer catalog; it simply removes the grouping. To remove an album you no longer need, follow these steps:

① In the Albums palette, right-click the album you want to remove.

② In the menu that appears, click **Delete**.

The Organizer displays a message box asking you to confirm the deletion.

③ Click **OK**.

The Organizer removes the album.

Create a Smart Album

A smart album has special criteria that determine what Photoshop Elements adds to the album. You can create smart albums for particular dates, tags, camera models, file sizes, and more.

The Organizer starts with a default smart album containing all photos taken in the past six months.

Create a Smart Album

① Open the Albums palette in the Organizer bin.

② Click plus (**+**) and then click **New Smart Album**.

The New Smart Album dialog box opens.

③ Type a name for your smart album.

④ Click here and choose a photo attribute.

⑤ Click here and choose a limiting factor.

⑥ Select or type the criterion for the attribute.

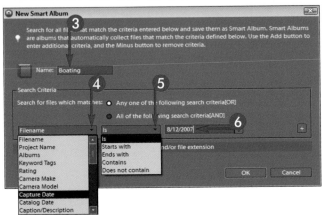

● You can click plus (+) to add additional criteria.

● If your smart album includes more than one criterion, you can specify whether the album requires any or all of the criteria to be met.

7 Click **OK**.

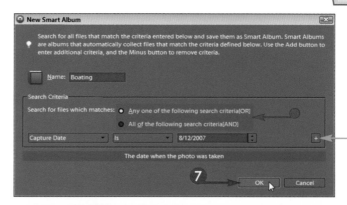

Photoshop Elements automatically adds photos that meet the criteria to the smart album and displays the album in the Photo Browser.

As you add more photos to your catalog, photos that meet the criteria are automatically added to the smart album.

TIP

How can I create a smart album using the Find feature?

You can find photos in the Organizer and then create a smart album based on the search criteria. The photos in the search results will be added to the new album.

1 Click **Find** and perform a search for photos in the current catalog.

Note: See the section "Find Photos" for more about searching for photos in the Organizer.

2 In the results list that appears, click **Options**.

3 Click **Save Search Criteria as Smart Album**.

Photoshop Elements creates a new smart album based on the search criteria.

View Photos by Date

To help you keep track of your photos, the Organizer can sort your images by date and display those that were taken in a specific date range. You can also view the images for a particular date range as a slide show.

View Photos by Date

① In the Organizer, click **Display**.

② Click **Date View**.

The Organizer displays a calendar view of your catalog.

● You can view your photos by year, month, or day. In this example, the Month view is displayed.

● To see a different month, click the **Previous Month** (◄) or **Next Month** (►) button.

③ Click the date for the photos you want to view.

● The first photo in the group appears here.

④ Click the **Play** button (►).

The Organizer starts a slide show, displaying each photo from the date you selected.

● To pause or stop the sequencing, click the **Pause** button ( ).

To view the previous image again, click the **Previous Item** button ( ).

To view the next image, click the **Next Item** button ( ).

⑤ Click **Find in the Photo Browser** ( ).

● The Photo Browser appears with the photo from the Date View selected.

You can also get to the Photo Browser from the Date View by clicking **Display** and then **Photo Browser**.

What is the Organizer timeline?

In the Photo Browser, you can browse photos by date by clicking and dragging along a timeline.

① Click **Window**.

② Click **Timeline**.

The timeline opens at the top of the Photo Browser.

● Click and drag the slider to move to a different photo date in the Photo Browser.

● Click and drag the end points to limit the range of dates displayed in the Photo Browser.

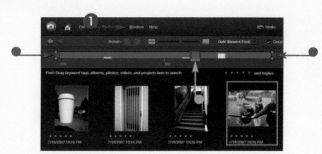

Work with Keyword Tags

Keyword tags help you categorize and filter your digital photos. You can assign the Organizer's preset tags or tags you create. You can also assign more than one tag to a photo.

Preset tags include those for people, family, and friends. You can assign tags to categories and subcategories.

Work with Keyword Tags

CREATE A KEYWORD TAG

1. In the Organizer, open the **Keyword Tags** palette in the Organizer bin.

2. Click plus () and then click **New Keyword Tag**.

The Create Keyword Tag dialog box appears.

3. Click here and then click a category for the new tag.

④ Type a name for the keyword tag.

● You can add a note about the keyword tag here.

⑤ Click **OK**.

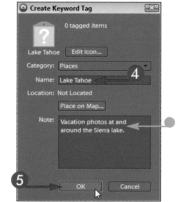

ASSIGN A TAG

⑥ Click and drag the tag from the Keyword Tags palette and drop it on the photo you want to tag.

The Organizer assigns the keyword tag. You can use the same drag-and-drop technique to assign preset keyword tags as well as tags you create.

You can also select multiple photos in the Organizer and drag them to the tag to assign a keyword tag.

● A keyword tag icon indicates that the photo has a tag assigned to it.

TIP

How do I edit a keyword tag?

① Right-click the keyword tag and click the **Edit Keyword Tag** command.

The Edit Keyword Tag dialog box opens.

② Type the keyword tag name or assign a new category to the tag.

③ Click **OK**.

Photoshop Elements applies the changes.

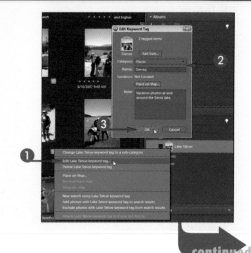

continued

After you assign keyword tags, you can filter your catalog to show only those photos that have certain tags. For example, you can filter your catalog to show only photos of people or events. You can also filter on multiple keyword tags at once.

Work with Keyword Tags *(continued)*

FILTER BY TAGS

1 In the Organizer, open the Keyword Tags palette if it is not already displayed.

2 Click the box next to the keyword tag on which you want to filter (■ changes to 🔲).

● You can click here (▶) to expand a tag category.

● You can click here (▼) to collapse a tag category.

To filter by more than one keyword tag, you can click additional tags.

● The Organizer displays the photos that share the keyword tag.

If you selected multiple tags, only photos that have all the tags display.

REMOVE A TAG FROM A PHOTO

1 Right-click the photo containing the tag you want to remove.

2 Click **Remove Keyword Tag**.

3 Click the keyword tag you want to remove.

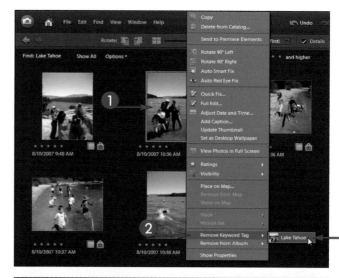

The Organizer removes the keyword tag.

TIP

How do I attach the same keyword tag to multiple photos?

1 In the Photo Browser, `Ctrl`-click the photos you want to tag.

2 Right-click the keyword tag and click **Attach keyword tag to selected items**.

The Organizer assigns the keyword tag to the selected photos.

You can use the Organizer's face-recognition feature to find the faces in your photos and display them for easy tagging. Elements automatically scans photos in the Organizer for the colors and structures that are characteristic of human faces.

You can create custom keyword tags in the People category for the friends and family members whose faces appear often in your photos.

Tag Faces

1 In the Organizer, open the Keyword Tags palette.

2 Click **Find Faces for Tagging** (📷).

You can optionally Ctrl-click photos in the Photo Browser first to limit your face search to those photos.

Elements searches for the faces in your photos and displays those faces in the Face Tagging dialog box.

3 Click a keyword tag and drag it to the face.

You can also Ctrl-click to select multiple faces and drag them to a keyword tag.

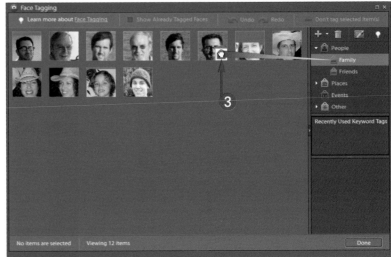

Elements applies the tag and hides the face in the dialog box.

● You can click to select **Show Already Tagged Faces** (■ changes to ☑) to display the tagged face again.

④ Repeat step **3** for the faces you want to tag.

⑤ Click **Done**.

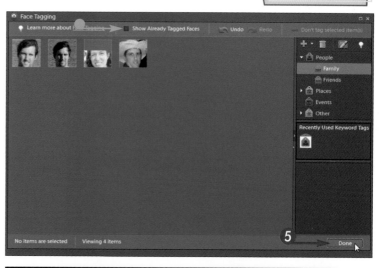

The photos with faces include the new tags.

TIP

How can I automatically find visually similar photos?

① In the Organizer, click to select a photo.

② Click **Find**.

③ Click **By Visual Similarity with Selected Photo(s)**.

Photoshop Elements displays similar photos in the organizer.

You can place your Organizer photos on a geographic map to specify where they were taken. The mapping feature in Photoshop Elements uses navigable-map technology from Yahoo!, allowing you to pan and zoom on the map and place your photos with precision.

You must have an active Internet connection for the mapping feature to work in Photoshop Elements.

Map a Photo

① Right-click a photo in the Organizer.

② Click **Place on Map**.

The Photo Location on Map dialog box appears.

③ Type a location for your photo.

In addition to specific addresses, cities, and states, you can type famous locations such as the Golden Gate Bridge or the Eiffel Tower.

④ Click **Find**.

Elements suggests one or more locations from its database.

⑤ Select a location.

⑥ Click **OK**.

- Elements displays a map with a red pointer () at the selected location.

- You can select the **Zoom In** tool ( ) and click the map to zoom in.

- You can select the **Zoom Out** tool ( ) and click the map to zoom out.

- You can select the **Hand** tool ( ) and click and drag the map to scroll.

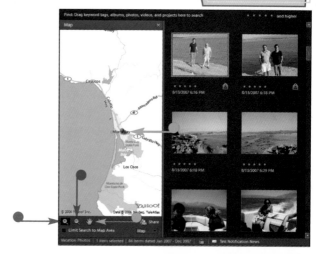

⑦ Zoom into the location using the map tools.

⑧ Click the red pointer ( ).

⑨ Click and drag the red pointer to a more specific location.

⑩ To close the map, click here.

TIP

How else can I add photos to the map?
With the Map window open, you can click and drag thumbnails to place photos on the map.

① In the Organizer, click **Display**.

② Click **Show Map**.

If an information box about mapping appears, click **OK**.

The Map window opens.

③ Click and drag a thumbnail to the map.

Elements maps the photo.

View Photo Properties

You can view the properties for any photo in your catalog. The Properties box displays a photo's general information, which includes the file name, file size, image size, and location. You can also view any associated tags, file history, and metadata information. Metadata, also known as EXIF data, is detailed information about how the photo was taken; it includes camera settings, such as exposure time and F-stop.

View Photo Properties

① In the Organizer, right-click a photo.

② Click **Show Properties**.

The Properties dialog box opens.

The General properties appear by default.

● You can add or edit a caption for the photo here.

● The size, capture date, and other information for the photo are shown here.

③ Click the **Metadata** button (⑤).

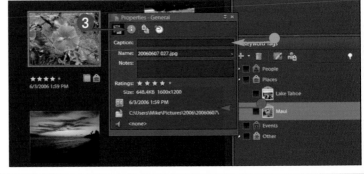

The Metadata properties appear. Metadata includes the camera model and settings if the photo came from a digital camera.

4 Click the **Keyword Tags** button (📇).

The Keyword Tags properties appear.

Elements displays any keyword tags or albums associated with the photo. You can right-click a tag or album to remove it from the photo.

● You can click the **History** button (📇) to view Organizer statistics for the photo.

5 Click here to close the Properties dialog box.

 TIP

How do I change the photo's date and time?
To change the date and time associated with a photo, follow these steps:

1 Right-click the photo you want to edit.

2 Click **Adjust Date and Time**.

The Adjust Date and Time dialog box opens.

3 Click to select the **Change to a specified date and time** option (● changes to ○).

4 Click **OK**.

5 In the Set Date and Time dialog box, set the new date and time.

6 Click **OK**.

Add a Caption

In the Organizer, you can add captions to your photos to help you remember important information about the images you catalog. For example, you may add captions to your vacation pictures with details about the location or subject matter. Captions appear below a photo when the image is viewed in Single Photo View.

Add a Caption

① In the Organizer, right-click the photo you want to caption.

② Click **Add Caption**.

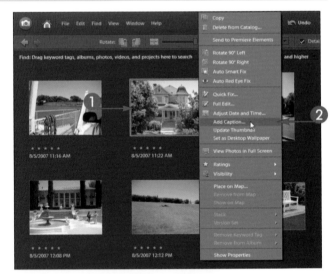

The Add Caption dialog box appears.

③ Type a caption for the photo.

④ Click **OK**.

The Organizer adds the caption to the photo.

⑤ Click the **Single Photo View** button ().

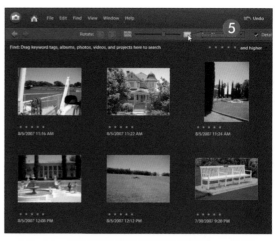

A larger version of the photo appears.

● The caption appears below the photo.

TIPS

Are there other ways to add captions to my photos?

Yes. You can also add captions to your photos using the Properties dialog box. See the section "View Photo Properties" for details.

How do I edit a caption?

To edit a caption, view the photo in Single Photo View in the Photo Browser window, click the caption, and make your changes. You can delete the caption completely, type a new caption, or make changes to the existing caption text. Press Enter to save your changes.

Find Photos

The Organizer offers a variety of methods for finding particular photos in your catalog. You can search for photos by date, file name, tags, and more.

In this example, you search for photos taken in a specific date range.

Find Photos

① In the Organizer, click **Find**.

② Click **Set Date Range**.

The Set Date Range dialog box opens.

③ Select the start date for the date range you want to search.

④ Select the end date for the date range you want to search.

⑤ Click **OK**.

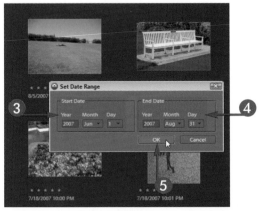

The Organizer displays any matching photos in the Photo Browser.

● A summary appears at the bottom of the Photo Browser.

RESET THE PHOTO BROWSER

❶ Click **Find**.

❷ Click **Clear Date Range**.

The Organizer resets the Photo Browser to include all the photos.

TIP

What other search methods can I use?

Here are some of the other ways to search the photos in the Organizer. You can access them from the Find menu.

By Caption or Note	Looks for photos based on the text of the notes and captions you have added to a photo.
By Filename	Searches the catalog for a particular file name.
By History	Looks up a photo based on when it was printed or e-mailed, or by other criteria.
By Media Type	Searches for creations, photos, and audio or video files in your catalog.
Items with Unknown Date or Time	Looks for photos lacking date or time data.
By Color Similarity with Selected Photos	Finds photos whose colors are similar to those of a selected photo.
Untagged Items	Searches for photos without assigned tags.
Items Not in Any Album	Displays items that are not associated with an album.

Stack Photos

In the Organizer, you can group similar photos into stacks. This can help you conserve space in the Organizer interface because stacks can be collapsed so that only the top photo on the stack appears. You can stack your photos manually, or have Elements suggest stacks based on photographic similarity.

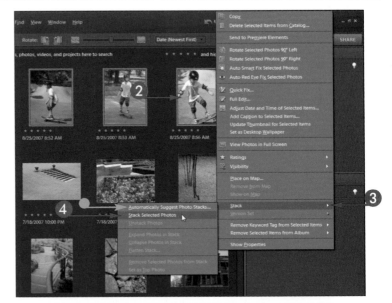

1. In the Organizer, Ctrl-click to select the photos you want to stack.

2. Right-click one of the selected photos.

3. Click **Stack**.

4. Click **Stack Selected Photos**.

● You can click **Automatically Suggest Photo Stacks** to have Elements suggest stacks based on photographic similarity.

● Photoshop Elements creates a stack for the selected photos. The photo that you right-clicked is placed on top of the stack and is displayed there.

5. Click to expand the stack ( ).

The stack expands to show its contents.

● You can click here to collapse the stack (◄Ⅱ).

UNSTACK PHOTOS

1 Right-click a photo in a stack. If the stack is collapsed, right-click the top photo.

2 Click **Stack**.

3 Click **Unstack Photos**.

Photoshop Elements removes the stack and places photos in the Organizer separately.

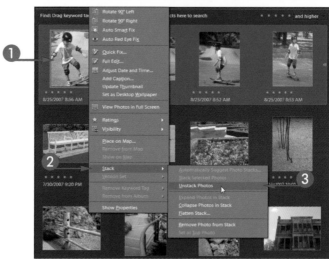

 TIP

How do I automatically stack photos as I import them?

You can have Photoshop Elements automatically group your photos into stacks by selecting an option in the Get Photos dialog box. The following steps show you how to do this when getting photos from a folder on your computer:

1 Click **File**.

2 Click **Get Photos and Videos**.

3 Click **From Files and Folders**.

4 In the dialog box that appears, click to select **Automatically Suggest Photo Stacks** (■ changes to ☑).

When you import the photos, Photoshop Elements suggests groups of photos to be stacked based on their photographic similarity.

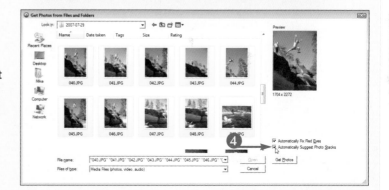

CHAPTER 4

Image Editing Basics

Are you ready to start working with images? This chapter shows you how to fine-tune your workspace. Discover how to change the on-screen image size, set a print size, and change the print resolution.

Work with Image Windows

Each image you open in Photoshop Elements appears in its own window. You can minimize and maximize image windows and tile multiple image windows in the workspace. If you have more than one image open, you can use the Project Bin to switch between image windows.

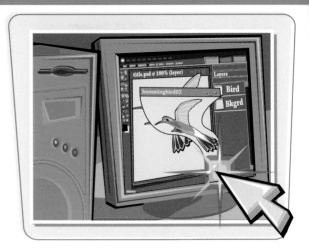

Work with Image Windows

① In the Editor, open two or more images.

Note: *For details about opening the Editor, see Chapter 1. See Chapter 2 for more on opening image files.*

● The active, or current, image appears here.

● The Photo Bin displays all the open images.

② Double-click the image you want to view.

● If your open images fill the Project Bin, you can use the scroll arrows to scroll to the image you want to view.

The image you select appears as the active image.

③ Click **Window**.

④ Click **Images**.

⑤ Click **Tile**.

Photoshop Elements displays all the open image files in individual windows in the workspace.

⑥ Click the **Close** button (⊠).

Photoshop Elements closes the image and resizes the other image windows.

● You can click the **Maximize** button (▢) to maximize an image in the workspace.

TIPS

Is there a way to close or hide the Project Bin or Palette Bin?

Yes. You can close the Project Bin and the Palette Bin to free up more workspace on-screen. To close the Project Bin, click the **Hide Project Bin** button (⬛). To close the Palette Bin, click the **Close Palette Bin** button (▶). To open either bin, click their respective buttons again. You can also open and close the bins using the **Window** menu.

Where else can I find commands for controlling my image windows?

You can click **Window** and then click **Images** to find a submenu of window commands. For example, you can cascade your open images across the workspace. If you are comparing several photos on-screen, you can click **Match Location** to view the same area in each open window. You can click **Match Zoom** to view each open window at the same zoom percentage.

menu
Window
image
match location
match zoom

Magnify with the Zoom Tool

You can change the magnification of an image with the Zoom tool. This enables you to view small details in an image or view an image at full size.

Magnify with the Zoom Tool

INCREASE MAGNIFICATION

1 In the Editor, click the **Zoom** tool (🔍).

Note: For details about opening the Editor, see Chapter 1.

2 Click the image.

Photoshop Elements increases the magnification of the image.

The point that you clicked in the image is centered in the window.

The current magnification shows in the image title bar and Options bar.

● You can select an exact magnification by typing a percentage value in the Options bar.

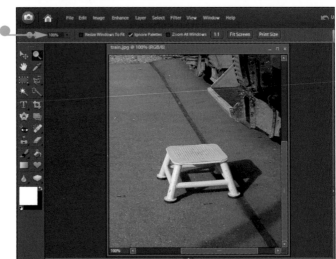

DECREASE MAGNIFICATION

1 Click the **Zoom Out** button (🔍).

2 Click the image.

Photoshop Elements decreases the magnification of the image.

MAGNIFY A DETAIL

1 Click the **Zoom In** button (🔍).

2 Click and drag with the **Zoom** tool to select the detail.

The area appears enlarged on-screen.

The more you zoom in, the more pixels you see and the less you see of the image's content.

TIP

How do I quickly return an image to 100% magnification?

The following are three different ways to return the image to 100% magnification:

1 By double-clicking the **Zoom** tool (🔍).

2 By clicking **1:1** in the Options bar.

3 By clicking **View** and then **Actual Pixels** from the menu.

You can move an image within a window by using the Hand tool or scroll bars. The Hand tool helps you navigate to an exact area in the image.

The Hand tool is a more flexible alternative to using the scroll bars because, unlike the scroll bars, the Hand tool enables you to drag the image freely in two dimensions.

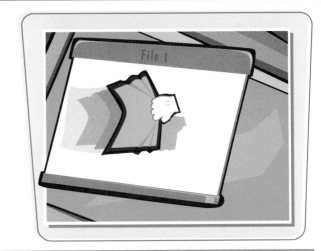

Adjust the Image View

USING THE HAND TOOL

1 In the Editor, click the **Hand** tool ( ).

Note: For details about opening the Editor, see Chapter 1.

Note: For the Hand tool ( ) to produce an effect, the image must be larger than the image window.

2 Click and drag inside the image window.

The view of the image shifts inside the window.

USING THE SCROLL BARS

1 Click and hold one of the window's scroll bar buttons (■, ■, ■, or ■).

The image scrolls in the direction you select.

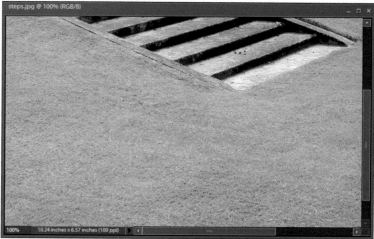

TIP

How can I quickly adjust the image window to see the entire image at its largest possible magnification on-screen?

The following are three different ways to magnify the image to its largest possible size:

1 By double-clicking the **Hand** tool (✋).

2 By clicking **Fit Screen** in the Options bar.

3 By clicking **View** and then **Fit on Screen**.

You can change the on-screen size of an image in Photoshop Elements by changing the image's pixel dimensions. This can enable you to fit an image on a Web page. Shrinking an image decreases its file size, which can make it easier to send by e-mail.

When you change an image's size, remember to resample. Resampling is the process of increasing or decreasing the number of pixels in an image.

Small

Large

Change the Image Size

1 In the Editor, click **Image**.

Note: For details about opening the Editor, see Chapter 1.

2 Click **Resize**.

3 Click **Image Size**.

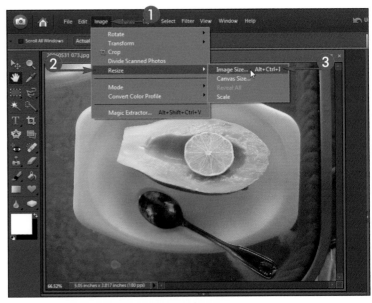

The Image Size dialog box appears, listing the width and height of the image in pixels.

● To resize by a certain percentage, click here and change the units to **percent**.

4 Click to select the **Resample Image** option (☐ changes to ✓).

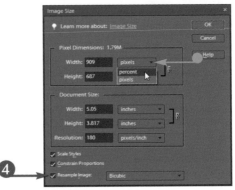

5 Type a size or percentage for a dimension.

● You can click to select the **Constrain Proportions** option (■ changes to ✓) to cause the other dimension to change proportionally.

6 Click **OK**.

You can restore the original dialog box settings without exiting the dialog box by holding down **Alt** and clicking **Cancel**, which changes to Reset.

Photoshop Elements resizes the image.

In this example, the image decreases to 50% of the original size.

Note: *Changing the number of pixels in an image can add blur. To sharpen a resized image, see Chapter 8.*

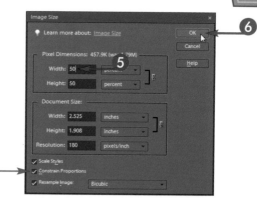

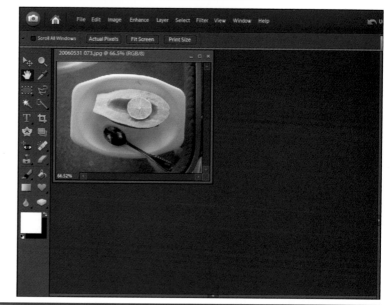

What is the difference between an image's on-screen size and its print size?

On-screen size depends only on the number of pixels that make up an image. Print size depends on the number of pixels as well as the print resolution, which is the density of the pixels on a printed page. Higher resolutions print a smaller image, and lower resolutions print a larger image, given the same on-screen size.

I do not like the new size I set. How do I undo the effect?

You can use the Undo and Redo commands in Photoshop Elements to undo an action you just performed, or redo an action you just undid. To undo an action, click the **Undo** button (🔄), or click **Edit** and then click **Undo**. To redo the action, click the **Redo** button (🔄), or click **Edit** and then click **Redo**. You can also use the Undo History palette. See the section "Undo Changes to an Image."

Change the Image Print Size

You can change the printed size of an image to determine how it appears on paper. Print size is also called *document size* in Photoshop Elements.

Change the Image Print Size

① In the Editor, click **Image**.

Note: For details about opening the Editor, see Chapter 1.

② Click **Resize**.

③ Click **Image Size**.

The Image Size dialog box appears, listing the current width and height of the printed image.

● You can click here to change the unit of measurement.

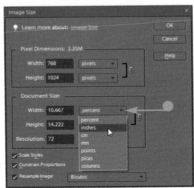

4 Type a size or percentage for a dimension.

● You can click to select the **Constrain Proportions** option (■ changes to ✓) to cause the other dimension to change proportionally.

5 Click **OK**.

You can restore the original dialog box settings by holding down Alt and clicking **Cancel**, which changes to Reset.

Photoshop Elements resizes the image.

Note: *Changing the size of an image can add blur. To sharpen a resized image, see Chapter 8.*

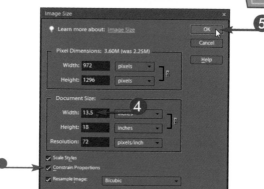

TIP

How do I preview an image's printed size?

1 Click **File**.

2 Click **Print**.

● The Print Preview dialog box shows how the image will print on the page.

● To select another print size, click here and click a print size.

3 Click **Print** to print the image.

Note: *For more about printing, see Chapter 16.*

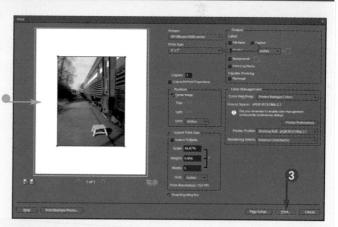

Change the Image Resolution

You can change the print resolution of an image to increase or decrease the print quality. The resolution, combined with the number of pixels in an image, determines the size of a printed image. The greater the resolution, the better the image looks on the printed page — up to a limit, which varies with the type of printer you use and the paper on which you are printing.

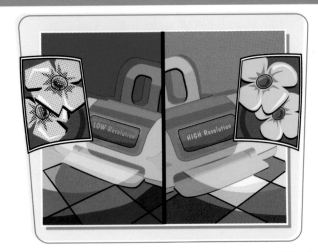

Change the Image Resolution

1. In the Editor, click **Image**.

Note: *For details about opening the Editor, see Chapter 1.*

2. Click **Resize**.

3. Click **Image Size**.

The Image Size dialog box appears, listing the current resolution of the image.

● You can click here to change the resolution units.

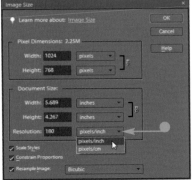

④ Type a new resolution.

● You can click to select the **Resample Image** option (☐ changes to ☑) to adjust the number of pixels in your image and keep the printed dimensions fixed.

⑤ Click **OK**.

You can restore the original dialog box settings by holding down Alt and clicking **Cancel**, which changes to Reset.

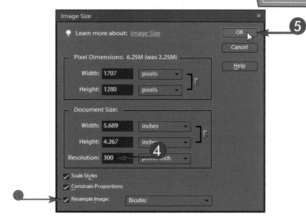

Photoshop Elements adjusts the image resolution.

If you checked Resample Image, the number of pixels changes, as does the on-screen image size.

 TIPS

What is the relationship between resolution, on-screen size, and print size?

To determine the printed size of a Photoshop Elements image, you can divide the on-screen size by the resolution. If you have an image with an on-screen width of 480 pixels and a resolution of 120 pixels per inch, the printed width is 4 inches.

What resolution should I use for images that I intend to print?

The appropriate resolution depends on a variety of factors, including the type of printer and paper you are using. However, for most standard inkjet printers, a resolution of 300 pixels per inch should be sufficient to produce good-quality prints on photo-quality paper. A resolution of 150 pixels per inch is sufficient for regular copier paper. Printing at lower resolutions may cause elements in your image to appear jagged.

Change the Image Canvas Size

You can alter the canvas size of an image to change its rectangular shape or add space around its borders. The canvas is the area on which an image sits. Changing the canvas size is one way to crop an image or add *matting*, which is blank space, around an image.

1 In the Editor, click **Image**.

Note: For details about opening the Editor, see Chapter 1.

2 Click **Resize**.

3 Click **Canvas Size**.

The Canvas Size dialog box appears, listing the current dimensions of the canvas.

● You can click here to change the unit of measurement.

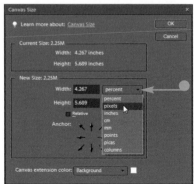

④ Type the new canvas dimensions.

● You can click an arrow () to determine in which directions Elements changes the canvas size. Selecting the square in the middle of the arrows crops the image equally on opposite sides.

⑤ Click **OK**.

*Note: If you decrease a dimension, Elements displays a dialog box asking whether you want to proceed. Click **Proceed**.*

Photoshop Elements changes the image's canvas size.

Elements fills any new canvas space with the background color — in this case, white.

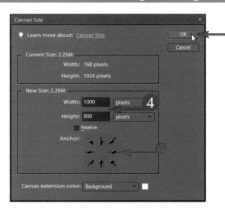

TIPS

Why would I want to change the canvas size instead of using the Crop tool?

You may find changing the canvas size useful when you want to reduce or enlarge your image by a certain number of inches, pixels, or other unit of measurement. The Crop tool (🔲) can be useful when you want to eliminate everything but a specific object in your image. The free-form nature of the Crop tool makes it easy to select specific objects. For more on cropping pictures, see Chapter 8.

How do I change the matte color around my canvas?

To add a color other than the default white to your canvas, you can click the Canvas extension color drop-down arrow (🔽) in the Canvas Size dialog box. This displays a menu from which you can choose another color, such as black or gray. You can click **Other** to select a color from the Elements color dialog box.

Undo Changes to an Image

You can undo commands using the Undo History palette. This enables you to correct mistakes or change your mind about operations you have performed on your image.

The Undo History palette lists recently executed commands, with the most recent command at the bottom.

Undo Changes to an Image

1. In the Editor, click **Window**.

Note: For details about opening the Editor, see Chapter 1.

2. Click **Undo History**.

   The Undo History palette opens.

3. Click the History slider (⬚) and drag it upward.

   ● Alternatively, you can click a previous command in the Undo History palette.

   ● Photoshop Elements undoes the previous commands.

   ● You can click and drag the slider down to redo the commands.

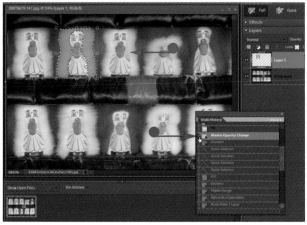

You can revert an image to the previously saved state. This enables you to start your image editing over.

Revert an Image

1 In the Editor, click **Edit**.

Note: For details about opening the Editor, see Chapter 1.

2 Click **Revert**.

Photoshop Elements reverts the image to its previously saved state.

● To return to the unreverted state, click **Edit** and then **Undo Revert**.

CHAPTER 5

Selection Techniques

Do you want to move, color, or transform parts of your image independently of the rest of the image? The first step is to make a selection. This chapter shows you how to use the Photoshop Elements selection tools to isolate portions of your images for editing.

Select an Area with a Marquee

You can select parts of an image for editing by using a marquee. You can then make changes to the selected area using other Photoshop Elements commands.

There are two versions of the Marquee tool. The Rectangular Marquee enables you to select square and rectangular shapes, and the Elliptical Marquee enables you to select circular or elliptical shapes.

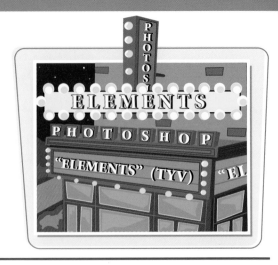

Select an Area with a Marquee

SELECT WITH THE RECTANGULAR MARQUEE

1. In the Editor, click the **Rectangular Marquee** tool (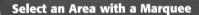).

Note: For details about opening the Editor, see Chapter 1.

2. Click and drag diagonally inside the image window.

   You can press and hold **Shift** while you click and drag to create a square selection.

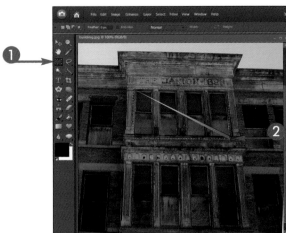

● Photoshop Elements selects a rectangular portion of your image.

   You can reposition selections by pressing the keyboard arrow keys (↑ , ↓ , ← , →).

● You can deselect a selection by clicking **Select** and then **Deselect** or by clicking outside the selection area.

SELECT WITH THE ELLIPTICAL MARQUEE

1 Click and hold the **Rectangular Marquee** tool ().

2 Click **Elliptical Marquee Tool** (▣).

3 Click and drag diagonally inside the image window.

You can press and hold Shift while you click and drag to create a circular selection or press Alt to draw the circle directly out from the center.

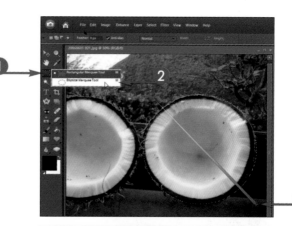

● Photoshop Elements selects an elliptical portion of your image.

You can reposition selections by pressing the keyboard arrow keys (↑, ↓, ←, →).

You can deselect a selection by clicking **Select** and then **Deselect** or by clicking outside the selection area.

TIP

How do I customize the Marquee tools?

You can customize the Marquee tools (▣ and ▣) by using the boxes and menus in the Options bar. Marquee options appear only when you click a Marquee tool.

Feather

Typing a Feather value softens your selection edge by making nearby pixels partially transparent. Use a feathered selection to blend selections that you move, cut, or copy.

Mode

The Mode list enables you to define your Marquee tool as a fixed size or aspect ratio.

Width and Height

You can also type an exact width and height for a fixed-size selection by entering values in the Width and Height boxes. These boxes are editable when you select a fixed-size or fixed-aspect-ratio marquee.

Select an Area with a Lasso

You can create oddly shaped selections with the Lasso tools. You can then make changes to the selected area by using other Photoshop Elements commands. You can use three types of Lasso tools: the regular Lasso, the Polygonal Lasso, and the Magnetic Lasso.

You can use the regular Lasso tool to create freehand selections. The Polygonal Lasso tool lets you easily create a selection made up of many straight lines.

Select an Area with a Lasso

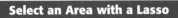

SELECT WITH THE REGULAR LASSO

1 In the Editor, click the **Lasso** tool (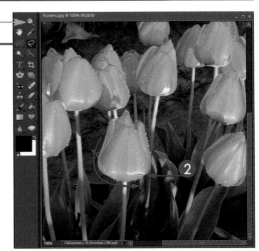).

Note: For details about opening the Editor, see Chapter 1.

2 Click and drag with your mouse pointer (◯) to make a selection.

● To accurately trace a complicated edge, you can magnify that part of the image with the Zoom tool (◯).

Note: See Chapter 4 for more on the Zoom tool.

3 Drag to the beginning point and release the mouse button.

Photoshop Elements completes the selection.

SELECT WITH THE POLYGONAL LASSO

① Click and hold the **Lasso** tool ().

② Click **Polygonal Lasso Tool** (⬡).

③ Click multiple times along the border of the area you want to select.

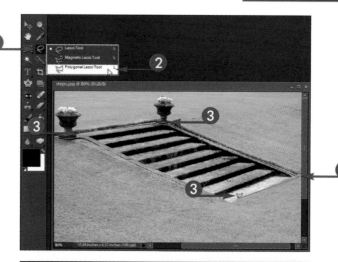

④ To complete the selection, click the starting point.

You can also double-click anywhere in the image. Photoshop Elements adds a final straight line connected to the starting point.

Photoshop Elements completes the selection.

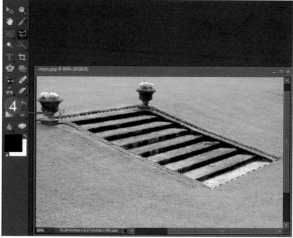

TIPS

How do I select all the pixels in my image?

You can use the Select All command to select everything in your image. Click **Select** and then click **All**. You can also press Ctrl + A on the keyboard. You can select all the pixels to perform an action on the entire image, such as copying the image.

What if my selection is not as precise as I want it to be?

You can deselect your selection by clicking **Select** and then **Deselect**. You can try to fix your selection; see the section "Add to or Subtract from a Selection." Or you can try switching to the Magnetic Lasso tool (⬡); see the following subsection, "Select with the Magnetic Lasso."

continued

You can quickly and easily select elements of your image that have well-defined edges with the Magnetic Lasso tool. The Magnetic Lasso works best when the element you are trying to select contrasts sharply with its background.

Select an Area with a Lasso *(continued)*

SELECT WITH THE MAGNETIC LASSO

① In the Editor, click and hold the **Lasso** tool (🔾).

Note: For details about opening the Editor, see Chapter 1.

② Click **Magnetic Lasso Tool** (🧲).

③ Click the edge of the object you want to select.

This creates a beginning anchor point.

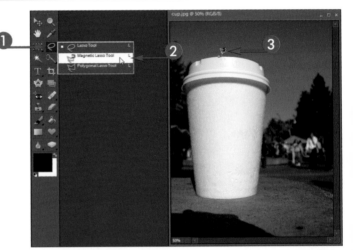

④ Drag your mouse pointer (🖉) along the edge of the object.

The Magnetic Lasso's path snaps to the edge of the element as you drag.

To help guide the lasso, you can click to add anchor points as you go along the path.

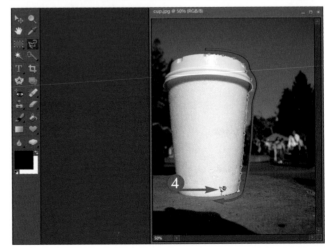

⑤ Click the beginning anchor point to finish your selection.

Alternatively, you can double-click anywhere in the image and Photoshop Elements will complete the selection for you.

The path is complete and the object is selected.

● This example shows that the Magnetic Lasso is less useful for selecting areas where there is little contrast between the image and its background.

 TIP

How can I adjust the precision of the Magnetic Lasso tool?
You can use the Options bar to adjust the Magnetic Lasso tool's precision:

Width
The number of nearby pixels the lasso considers when creating a selection.

Edge Contrast
How much contrast is required for the lasso to consider something an edge.

Frequency
The frequency of the anchor points.

Select an Area with the Magic Wand

You can select groups of similarly colored pixels with the Magic Wand tool. You may find this useful if you want to remove an object from a background.

By specifying an appropriate tolerance value, you can control how similar a pixel needs to be for Photoshop Elements to select it.

Select an Area with the Magic Wand

1 In the Editor, click the **Magic Wand** tool (✦).

Note: For details about opening the Editor, see Chapter 1.

The mouse pointer (◉) changes to a magic wand (✦).

2 Type a number from 0 to 255 into the Tolerance field.

To select a narrow range of colors, type a small number; to select a wide range of colors, type a large number.

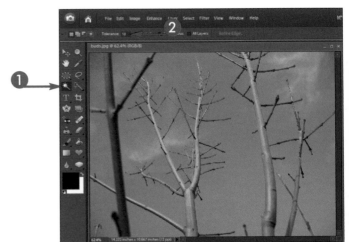

3 Click the area you want to select inside the image.

● Photoshop Elements selects the pixel you clicked, plus any similarly colored pixels near it.

● To select all the similar pixels in the image, not just the contiguous pixels, deselect the **Contiguous** check box (☑ changes to ■).

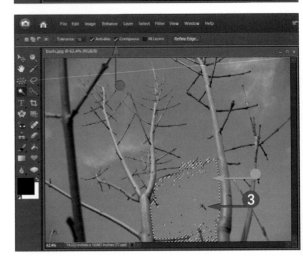

● This example shows a higher tolerance value, resulting in a greater number of similarly colored pixels selected in the image.

④ To add to your selection, press **Shift** and click elsewhere in the image.

Photoshop Elements adds to your selection.

● You can also click one of three selection buttons in the Options bar to grow or decrease the selection.

Note: For more on these buttons, see the section "Add to or Subtract from a Selection" later in this chapter.

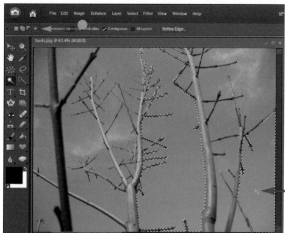

How can I help ensure that the Magic Wand tool selects all the instances of a color in an image?

You can deselect **Contiguous** (☑ changes to ■) in the Options bar so that the Magic Wand tool selects similar colors, even when they are not contiguous with the pixel you click with the tool. This can be useful when objects intersect the solid-color areas of your image. You can also select **All Layers** (■ changes to ☑) to select similar colors in all layers in the image, not just in the currently selected layer.

Select an Area with the Quick Selection Tool

You can paint selections onto your images using the Quick Selection tool. This tool offers a quick way to select objects that have solid colors and well-defined edges.

You can adjust the brush size of the tool to fine-tune your selections.

Select an Area with the Quick Selection Tool

1 In the Editor, click the **Quick Selection** tool (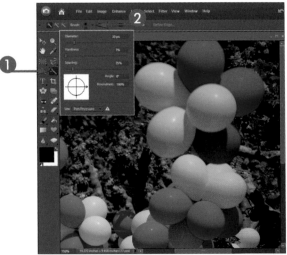).

Note: *For details about opening the Editor, see Chapter 1.*

2 Click here to open the tool's Brush menu.

The Brush menu opens.

In the Brush menu, you can specify the tool's size and other characteristics. Decreasing the tool's hardness causes it to partially select pixels at the perimeter.

3 Click and drag inside the object you want to select.

- Photoshop Elements selects parts of the object based on its coloring and the contrast of its edges.

- After you make a selection, the Add to Selection button () becomes active.

4 Click and drag to select more of the object.

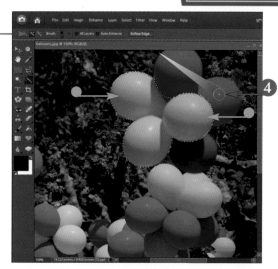

- Photoshop Elements adds to the selection.

How can I adjust a selection made with the Quick Selection tool?

1 In the Options bar, click **Refine Edge**.

The Refine Edge dialog box opens.

- You can increase **Smooth** to lessen the sharpness of any corners in your selection.

- You can increase **Feather** to make the edges of your selection partially transparent.

- You can use **Contract/Expand** to decrease or increase the selection slightly.

- You can click here to define your selection with a custom overlay color.

Select an Area with the Selection Brush

You can select oddly shaped areas in your image by painting with the Selection Brush. By customizing the size and hardness of the brush, you can accurately trace edges that are curved or not well defined.

Select an Area with the Selection Brush

SELECT WITH THE SELECTION BRUSH

① In the Editor, click and hold the **Quick Selection** tool (🖌).

Note: For details about opening the Editor, see Chapter 1.

② Click **Selection Brush Tool** (🖌).

③ Click here.

A slider (🔲) appears.

④ Click and drag the slider to specify a size.

You can also type a size.

⑤ Type a hardness from 0 to 100%.

A smaller value produces a softer selection edge.

⑥ Click here and then click **Selection**.

⑦ Click and drag to paint a selection.

⑧ Click and drag multiple times to paint over the area you want to select.

Photoshop Elements creates a selection.

You can change the brush settings as you paint to select different types of edges in your object.

DESELECT WITH THE SELECTION BRUSH

① Click the **Selection Brush** tool ().

② Press and hold Alt.

③ Click and drag where you want to remove the selection area.

Photoshop Elements removes the selection.

TIP

How do I paint a mask with the Selection Brush?

The Selection Brush's Mask option enables you to define the area that is selected using a partially transparent color. One advantage of using a mask is that it lets you see the soft edges painted by a soft selection brush.

① Click the drop-down arrow (▾) in the Options bar and then click **Mask**.

② Click and drag to define the mask.

By default, the masked area shows up as a see-through red color called a rubylith.

To turn a painted mask into a selection, click the drop-down arrow (▾) in the Options bar and then click **Selection**.

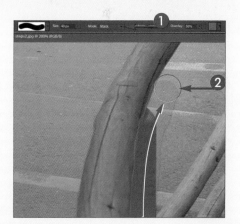

Add to or Subtract from a Selection

You can add to or subtract from your selection by using various selection tool options.

See the previous sections in this chapter to find out how to choose the appropriate tool for selecting elements in your photo.

Add to or Subtract from a Selection

ADD TO YOUR SELECTION

1. In the Editor, make a selection using one of the selection tools.

Note: For details about opening the Editor, see Chapter 1.

2. Click a selection tool.

   This example uses the Lasso tool ().

3. Click the **Add to Selection** button (▢).

4. Select the area you want to add.

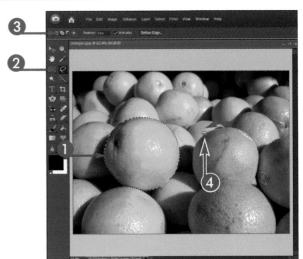

5. Complete the selection.

   Elements adds to the selection.

   You can enlarge the selection further by repeating steps **2** to **5**.

   You can also add to a selection by pressing Shift as you select an area.

SUBTRACT FROM YOUR SELECTION

① Make a selection using one of the selection tools.

② Click a selection tool.

The selection in this example illustrates the use of the Rectangular Marquee tool (▦).

③ Click the **Subtract from Selection** button (▣).

④ Select the area you want to subtract.

● Photoshop Elements deselects, or subtracts, the selected area.

You can subtract other parts of the selection by repeating steps **2** to **4**.

You can also subtract from a selection by pressing Alt as you select an area.

TIPS

How do I add to or subtract from a selection using the Quick Selection tool?

The Quick Selection tool (🖌) features buttons for adding to or subtracting from a selection. In the Options bar, you can click the **Add to Quick Selection** button (🖌) to add to a selection and the **Subtract from Quick Selection** button (🖌) to subtract from a selection.

Can I move the selection marquee without moving the item selected?

Yes. Use any of the selection tools to select an area and then press an arrow key (⬆, ⬇, ⬅, ➡) to move the selection in 1-pixel increments. Press and hold Shift while pressing an arrow key to move the selection in 10-pixel increments. This technique is handy when you need to nudge the marquee slightly across your image.

Save and Load a Selection

You can save a selected area in your image to reuse later. This can be useful if you anticipate future edits to the same part of your image. You can load the saved selection instead of having to reselect it.

See the previous sections in this chapter to read more about choosing the appropriate tool for selecting areas in your image.

Save and Load a Selection

SAVE A SELECTION

1 In the Editor, make a selection using one of the selection tools.

Note: For details about opening the Editor, see Chapter 1.

2 Click **Select**.

3 Click **Save Selection**.

The Save Selection dialog box opens.

4 Make sure **New** is selected in the Selection field.

New is the default setting.

5 Type a name for the selection.

6 Click **OK**.

Elements saves the selection.

LOAD A SELECTION

① Click **Select**.

② Click **Load Selection**.

Note: See the subsection "Save a Selection" to learn how to save your selection.

The Load Selection dialog box opens.

③ Click here and then click the saved selection you want to load.

④ Click **OK**.

● The selection appears in the image.

How can I modify a saved selection?

You can modify a saved selection by making a new selection in your image window, completing steps **2** and **3** of "Save a Selection" to open the Save Selection dialog box, and then choosing the selection you want to modify from the Selection menu. The Operation radio buttons enable you to replace, add to, subtract from, or intersect with your selection. Choosing **Intersect** (●) keeps any area where the new selection and the saved selection overlap. Click **OK** to modify your saved selection.

Invert a Selection

You can invert a selection to deselect what is currently selected and select everything else. This is useful when you want to select the background around an object.

Invert a Selection

1. In the Editor, make a selection using one of Photoshop Elements' selection tools.

Note: For details about opening the Editor, see Chapter 1. For more about the various selection tools, see the previous sections in this chapter.

2. Click **Select**.

3. Click **Inverse**.

● Photoshop Elements inverts the selection.

Deselect a Selection

You can deselect a selection when you are done manipulating what is inside it or if you make a mistake and want to try selecting again.

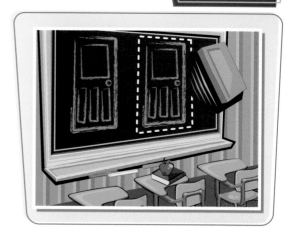

Deselect a Selection

① In the Editor, make a selection using one of Photoshop Elements' selection tools.

Note: *For details about opening the Editor, see Chapter 1. For more about the various selection tools, see the previous sections in this chapter.*

   In this example, several flowers are selected.

② Click **Select**.

③ Click **Deselect**.

   Photoshop Elements cdeselects the selection.

CHAPTER 6

Manipulating Selections

Making a selection in Photoshop Elements isolates a specific area of your image. This chapter shows you how to move, stretch, erase, and manipulate your selection in a variety of ways.

Move a Selection

You can rearrange elements of your image by moving selections with the Move tool. You can move elements of your image either in the default Background layer or in other layers you create for your image.

If you move elements in the Background layer, Photoshop Elements fills the original location with the current background color. If you move elements in another layer, Elements makes the original location transparent, revealing any underlying layers. See Chapter 7 for more on layers.

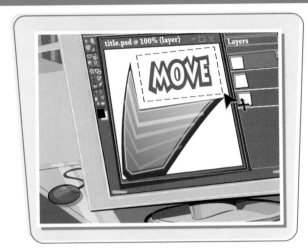

Move a Selection

MOVE A SELECTION IN THE BACKGROUND

① In the Editor, display the Layers palette.

Note: For details about opening the Editor or opening palettes, see Chapter 1.

② Click the Background layer.

A newly imported image has only a Background layer.

Note: See Chapter 7 for more on layers.

③ Make a selection with a selection tool.

Note: For more about selecting elements, see Chapter 5.

④ Click the **Move** tool ().

⑤ Click inside the selection and drag.

● Photoshop Elements fills the original location of the selection with the current background color.

● In this example, white is the default background color.

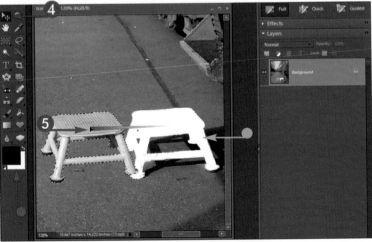

MOVE A SELECTION IN A LAYER

1. Click a layer in the Layers palette.

Note: *See Chapter 7 for more on layers.*

In this example, the layer contains an element from a different photo.

2. Make a selection with a selection tool.

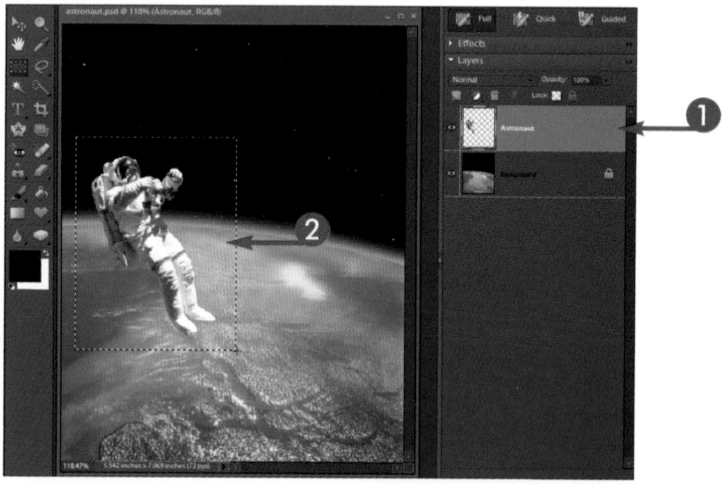

3. Click the **Move** tool.
4. Click inside the selection and drag.

Photoshop Elements moves the selection and fills the original location of the selection with transparent pixels.

Note: *Unlike the Background — Elements' opaque default layer — other layers can include transparent pixels.*

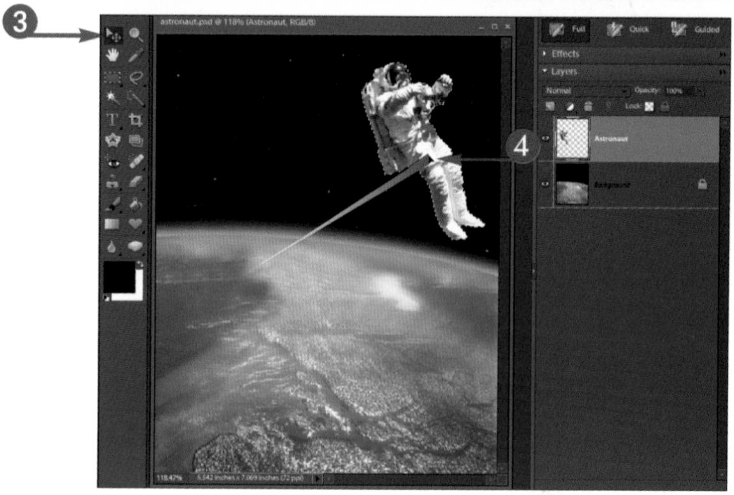

TIPS

How do I move a selection in a straight line?

Press and hold the Shift key while you drag with the Move tool. Doing so constrains the movement of your selection horizontally, vertically, or diagonally depending on the direction you drag.

How do I move several layers at a time?

You can link the layers you want to move, select one of the linked layers, and then move them all with the Move tool. For more information, see the section "Link Layers" in Chapter 7. You can also Ctrl-click to select multiple layers in the Layers palette. Use the Move tool to move the selected layers.

Copy and Paste a Selection

You can copy a selection and make a duplicate of it somewhere else in the image. You may use this technique to retouch an element in your photo by placing good content over bad.

Copy and Paste a Selection

① In the Editor, make a selection with a selection tool.

Note: For details about opening the Editor, see Chapter 1.

Note: See Chapter 5 for more on using selection tools.

② Click the **Move** tool (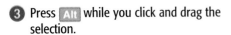).

● You can also click **Copy** and **Paste** in the Edit menu to copy and paste selections.

③ Press Alt while you click and drag the selection.

④ Release the mouse button to drop the selection into place.

Photoshop Elements creates a duplicate of the selection and moves it to the new location.

Delete a Selection

You can delete a selection to remove unwanted elements from an image. If you delete an element from the Background layer, Elements replaces the original location with the current background color. If you delete a selection in another layer, Elements replaces the selection with transparent pixels, and any underlying layers show through.

Delete a Selection

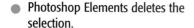

① In the Editor, make a selection with a selection tool.

Note: *For details about opening the Editor, see Chapter 1. See Chapter 5 for more on using selection tools.*

② Press Delete.

● Photoshop Elements deletes the selection.

If you are working in the Background layer, the original location fills with the background color — in this example, white.

If you are working in a layer other than the Background layer, deleting a selection turns the selected pixels transparent, and layers below it show through.

Rotate a Selection

You can rotate a selection to tilt an element or turn it upside down in your image. You may rotate an element to create a better composition or to correct the appearance of an element.

When you rotate a selection in the Background layer, Photoshop Elements replaces the exposed areas that the rotation creates with the current background color. If you rotate a selection in another layer, the underlying layers appear in the exposed areas. See Chapter 7 for more on layers.

Rotate a Selection

① In the Editor, make a selection with a selection tool.

Note: For details about opening the Editor, see Chapter 1.

In this example, content in a layer is selected.

Note: See Chapter 5 for more on using selection tools and Chapter 7 for more on layers.

② Click **Image**.

③ Click **Rotate**.

④ Click **Free Rotate Selection**.

You can click other commands in the Rotate menu to rotate your selection in a more constrained way.

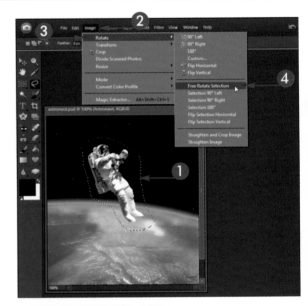

⑤ Click and drag a rotation handle.

The selection rotates.

⑥ Click ✔ or press Enter to apply the rotation.

● You can click ⊘ or press Esc to cancel.

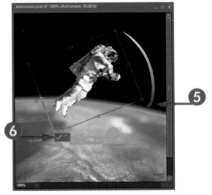

You can scale a selection to make it larger or smaller. Scaling enables you to adjust or emphasize parts of your image.

When you scale a selection in the Background layer, Photoshop Elements replaces the exposed areas that the scaling creates with the current background color. If you scale a selection in another layer, the underlying layers appear in the exposed areas. See Chapter 7 for more on layers.

Scale a Selection

① In the Editor, make a selection with a selection tool.

Note: For details about opening the Editor, see Chapter 1.

In this example, content in a layer is selected.

Note: See Chapter 5 for more on using selection tools and Chapter 7 for more on layers.

② Click **Image**.

③ Click **Resize**.

④ Click **Scale**.

A box with handles on the sides and corners surrounds the selection.

⑤ Drag a handle to scale the selection.

Drag a corner handle to scale both the horizontal and vertical axes.

● With Constrain Proportions selected (■ changes to ✓), the height and width change proportionally.

⑥ Click ✓ or press Enter to apply the scale effect.

● You can click ⊘ or press Esc to cancel.

Photoshop Elements scales the selection.

Skew or Distort a Selection

You can transform a selection using the Skew or Distort command. This lets you stretch elements in your image into interesting shapes.

When you skew or distort a selection in the Background layer, Photoshop Elements replaces the exposed areas that the skewing or distorting creates with the current background color. If you skew or distort a selection in another layer, the underlying layers appear in the exposed areas. See Chapter 7 for more on layers.

Fig. 3, Skew the Selection.

Skew or Distort a Selection

SKEW A SELECTION

① In the Editor, make a selection with a selection tool.

Note: For details about opening the Editor, see Chapter 1. See Chapter 5 for more on using selection tools.

② Click **Image**.

③ Click **Transform**.

④ Click **Skew**.

A rectangular box with handles on the sides and corners surrounds the selection.

⑤ Click and drag a handle.

Photoshop Elements skews the selection.

Because the Skew command works along a single axis, you can drag either horizontally or vertically.

⑥ Click ✔ or press `Enter` to apply the skewing.

● You can click ⊘ or press `Esc` to cancel.

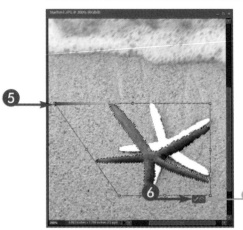

DISTORT A SELECTION

1. Make a selection with a selection tool.
2. Click **Image**.
3. Click **Transform**.
4. Click **Distort**.

A rectangular box with handles on the sides and corners surrounds the selection.

5. Click and drag a handle.

Photoshop Elements distorts the selection.

The Distort command works independently of the selection's axes; you can drag a handle both vertically and horizontally.

6. Click ☑ or press [Enter] to apply the distortion.

● You can click ⊘ or press [Esc] to cancel.

 TIP

Can I perform several transforming effects at once to a selection?

1. Click **Image**.
2. Click **Transform**.
3. Click **Free Transform**.
4. Drag a handle on the box that surrounds the selection to transform it.

● You can switch between transformation operations by clicking these buttons.

5. Click ☑ or press [Enter] to apply the effect.

Feather the Border of a Selection

You can feather a selection's border to create soft edges. Feathering enables you to control the sharpness of the edges in a selection. You can use this technique with other layers to create a blending effect between the selected area and any underlying layers.

To create a soft edge around an object, you must first select the object, feather the selection border, and then delete the part of the image that surrounds your selection.

Feather the Border of a Selection

FEATHER A SELECTION

1 In the Editor, make a selection with a selection tool.

Note: For details about opening the Editor, see Chapter 1. See Chapter 5 for more on using selection tools.

2 Click **Select**.

3 Click **Feather**.

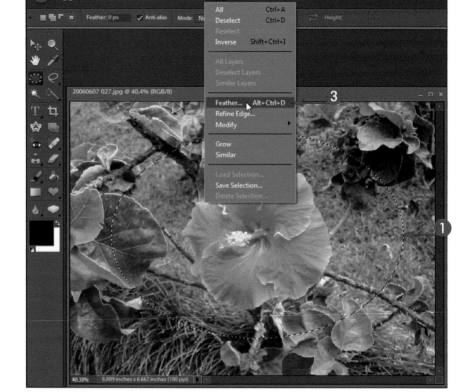

The Feather Selection dialog box appears.

4 Type a pixel value between 0.2 and 250 to determine the softness of the edge.

5 Click **OK**.

DELETE THE SURROUNDING BACKGROUND

1 Click **Select**.

2 Click **Inverse**.

The selection inverts but remains feathered.

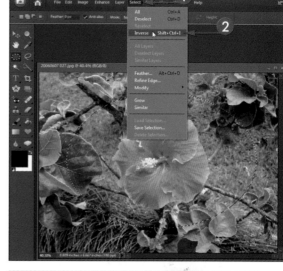

3 Press Delete.

If you are working with the Background layer, the deleted area is filled with the current background color.

If you are working with a layer other than the Background layer, the deleted area becomes transparent and the layers below show through.

You can now see the effect of the feathering.

TIPS

How do I feather my selection into a colored background?

You can add a solid-color fill layer behind your photo and blend the feathered selection into the new layer. The layer containing the selection appears on top of the solid-color fill layer, and the feathering technique creates a softened blend between the two layers. For more on creating a fill layer, see Chapter 7.

What happens if I feather a selection and then apply a command to it?

Photoshop Elements applies the command only partially to pixels near the edge of the selection. For example, if you are removing color from a selection using the Hue/Saturation command, color at the feathered edge of the selection is only partially removed. For more information about the Hue/Saturation command, see Chapter 10.

CHAPTER 7

Layer Basics

You can separate the elements in your image so that you can move and transform them independently of one another. You can accomplish this by placing them in different layers.

A Photoshop Elements image can consist of multiple layers, with each layer containing different objects in the image.

When you open a digital-camera photo or a newly scanned image in Elements, it exists as a single layer known as the Background layer. You can add new layers on top of the Background layer as you work.

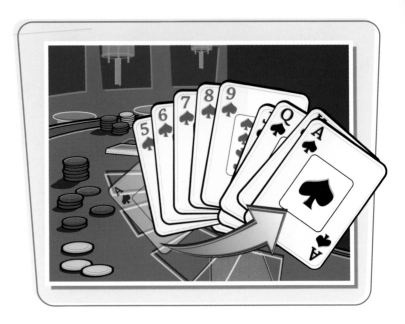

Layer Independence

Layered Photoshop Elements files act like several images combined into one. Each layer of an image has its own set of pixels that you can move and transform independently of the pixels in other layers.

Apply Commands to Layers

Most Photoshop Elements commands affect only the layer that you select. For example, if you click and drag using the Move tool (), the selected layer moves while the other layers stay in place. If you apply a color adjustment, only colors in the selected layer change.

Manipulate Layers

You can combine, duplicate, and hide layers in an image and shuffle their order. You can also link particular layers so that they move in unison, or blend content from different layers in creative ways. You manage all this in the Layers palette.

Transparency

Layers can have transparent areas, where the elements in the layers below can show through. When you perform a cut or erase command on a layer, the affected pixels become transparent. You can also make a layer partially transparent by decreasing its opacity.

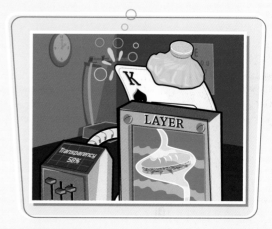

Adjustment Layers

Adjustment layers are special layers that contain information about color or tonal adjustments. An adjustment layer affects the pixels in all the layers below it. You can increase or decrease an adjustment layer's intensity to get precisely the effect you want.

Save Layered Files

You can save multilayered images only in Photoshop, PDF, and TIFF file formats. To save a layered image in another file format — for example, PICT, BMP, GIF, or JPEG — you must combine the image's layers into a single layer, a process known as flattening. For more information about saving files, see Chapter 16.

Create and Add to a Layer

To keep elements in your image independent of one another, you can create separate layers and add objects to them.

CREATE A LAYER

1. In the Editor, display the Layers palette.

Note: For details about opening the Editor or opening palettes, see Chapter 1.

2. Click the layer above which you want to add the new layer.

3. In the Layers palette, click the **Create a New Layer** button (■).

   Alternatively, you can click **Layer**, **New**, and then **Layer**.

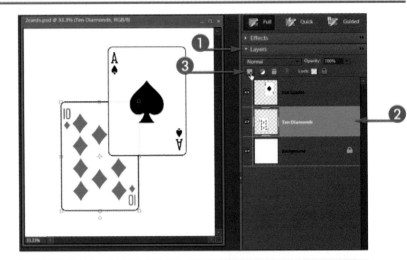

● Photoshop Elements creates a new, transparent layer.

Note: To change the name of a layer, see the section "Rename a Layer."

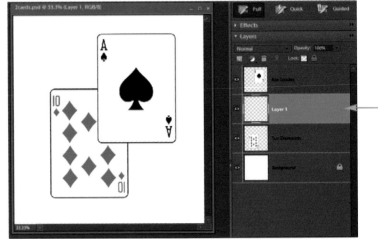

COPY AND PASTE INTO A LAYER

Note: *This example shows how to add content to the new layer by copying and pasting from another image file.*

1 Open another image.

2 Using a selection tool, select the content you want to copy into the other image.

Note: *See Chapter 1 for more about opening an image; see Chapter 5 for more about the selection tools.*

3 Click **Edit**.

4 Click **Copy**.

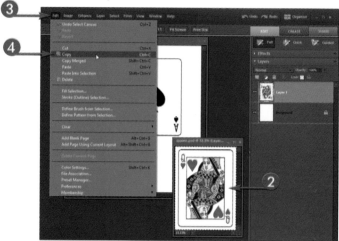

5 Click the image window where you created the new layer.

6 Click the new layer in the Layers palette.

7 Click **Edit**.

8 Click **Paste**.

● The selected content from the other image appears in the new layer.

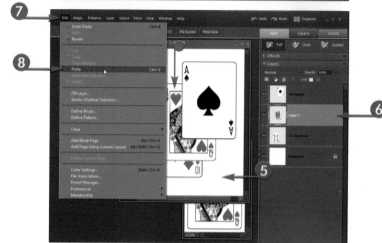

TIPS

What is the Background layer?

The Background layer is the default bottom layer. It appears when you create a new image that has a nontransparent background color, or when you import an image from a scanner or digital camera. You can create new layers on top of a Background layer but not below it. Unlike other layers, a Background layer cannot contain transparent pixels.

How do I turn the Background layer into a regular layer?

If you have the Background layer selected, you can click **Layer**, **New**, and then **Background from Layer** to turn it into a regular layer. The converted layer can be edited just like any other layer.

You can hide a layer to temporarily remove elements in that layer from view.

Hidden layers do not appear when you print or use the Save for Web command.

Hide a Layer

① In the Editor, display the Layers palette.

Note: For details about opening the Editor or opening palettes, see Chapter 1.

② Click a layer.

③ Click the **Layer Visibility** icon (👁) for the layer.

The icon disappears.

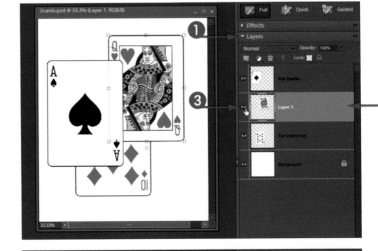

Photoshop Elements hides the layer.

● A bounding box shows where the hidden layer's content is located.

To show one layer and hide all the others, you can press **Alt** and click the **Layer Visibility** icon (👁) for the layer you want to show.

Note: You can also delete a layer. See the section "Delete a Layer" for more information.

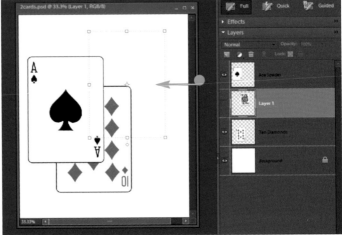

Move a Layer

You can use the Move tool to reposition the elements in one layer without moving those in others.

Move a Layer

1 In the Editor, display the Layers palette.

Note: *For details about opening the Editor or opening palettes, see Chapter 1.*

2 Click a layer.

3 Click the **Move** tool ().

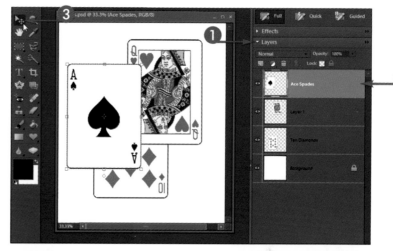

4 Click and drag inside the window.

Content in the selected layer moves.

Content in the other layers does not move.

Note: *To move several layers at the same time, see the section "Link Layers."*

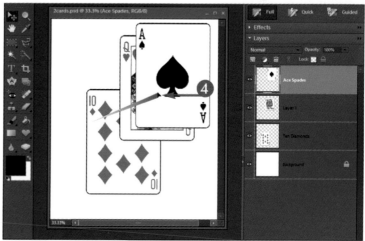

By duplicating a layer, you can manipulate elements in an image while keeping a copy of their original state.

Duplicate a Layer

① In the Editor, display the Layers palette.

Note: For details about opening the Editor or opening palettes, see Chapter 1.

② Click a layer.

③ Click and drag the layer to the **Create a New Layer** button (■).

Alternatively, you can click **Layer** and then **Duplicate Layer**; a dialog box appears, asking you to name the layer you want to duplicate.

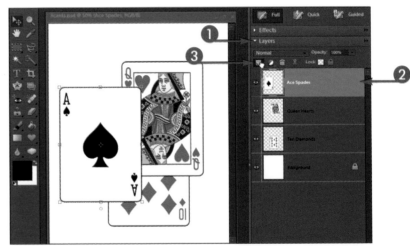

● Photoshop Elements duplicates the selected layer.

Note: To rename the duplicate layer, see the section "Rename a Layer."

● You can test that Photoshop Elements has duplicated the layer by selecting the new layer, clicking the **Move** tool (▶), and clicking and dragging the layer.

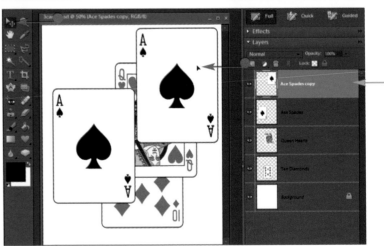

You can delete a layer when you
no longer have a use for its
contents.

Delete a Layer

1 In the Editor, display the Layers palette.

*Note: For details about opening the Editor or opening
palettes, see Chapter 1.*

2 Click a layer.

3 Click and drag the layer to the **Trash**
icon (🗑).

Alternatively, you can click **Layer** and
then **Delete Layer**, or you can select a
layer and click the **Trash** icon (🗑). In
both cases, a confirmation dialog box
appears.

Photoshop Elements deletes the
selected layer, and the content in the
layer disappears from the image
window.

*Note: You can also hide a layer. See the section "Hide a
Layer" for more information.*

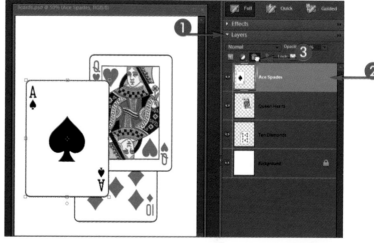

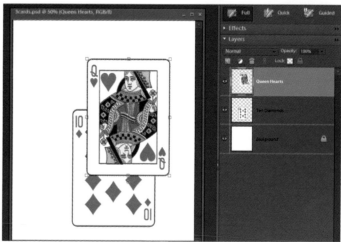

Reorder Layers

You can change the stacking order of layers to move elements forward or backward in your image.

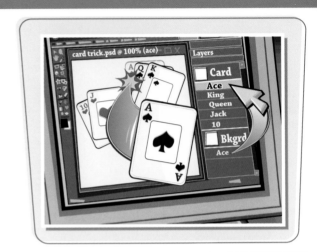

USING THE LAYERS PALETTE

① In the Editor, display the Layers palette.

Note: *For details about opening the Editor or opening palettes, see Chapter 1.*

② Click a layer.

③ Click and drag the layer to change its arrangement in the stack.

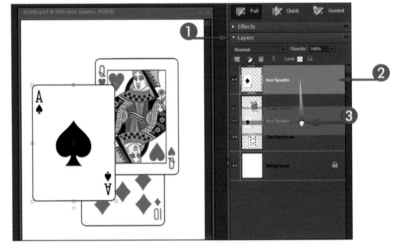

● The layer assumes its new position in the stack.

● In this example, the Ace Spades layer moves down in the stack.

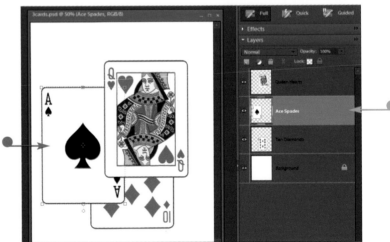

USING THE ARRANGE COMMANDS

① Click a layer.

② Click **Layer**.

③ Click **Arrange**.

④ Click the command for how you want to move the layer.

You can select Bring to Front, Bring Forward, Send Backward, Send to Back, or Reverse.

Note: *Reverse is available only if more than one layer is selected. You can* Ctrl *-click in the Layers palette to select multiple layers.*

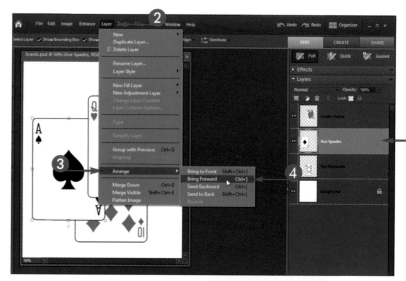

In this example, Bring Forward is selected.

● The layer assumes its new position in the stack.

◉ In this example, the Ace Spades layer moves to the top of the stack.

Note: *You cannot move a layer in back of the default Background layer.*

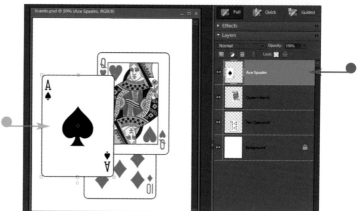

Are there shortcuts for changing the order of layers?

You can shift layers forward and backward in the stack by pressing the following shortcut keys:

Move...	Shortcut
...forward one step	Ctrl +]
...backward one step	Ctrl + [
...to the very front	Shift + Ctrl +]
...to the very back	Shift + Ctrl + [

Change the Opacity of a Layer

You can adjust the opacity of a layer to let elements in the layers below show through. Opacity is the opposite of transparency — decreasing the opacity of a layer increases its transparency.

Change the Opacity of a Layer

1 In the Editor, display the Layers palette.

Note: For details about opening the Editor or opening palettes, see Chapter 1.

2 Click the layer whose opacity you want to change.

Note: You cannot change the opacity of the Background layer.

● The default opacity is 100%, which is completely opaque.

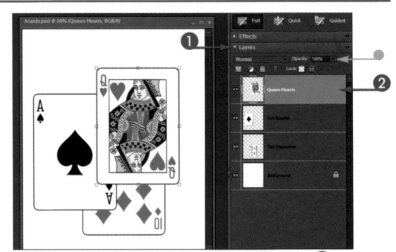

3 Type a new value in the Opacity field.

● Alternatively, you can click here and then drag the selection slider (▣).

A layer's opacity can range from 0% to 100%.

● The layer changes in opacity.

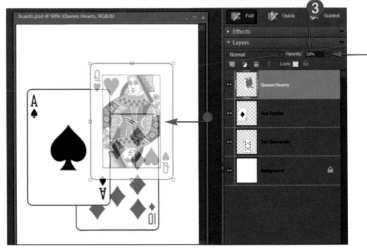

Linking causes different layers to move in unison when you move them with the Move tool. You may find linking useful when you want to keep elements of an image aligned with one another but do not want to merge their layers. Keeping layers unmerged lets you apply effects to each layer independently.

See the section "Merge Layers" for more on merging. For more on moving a layer, see the section "Move a Layer."

Link Layers

① In the Editor, display the Layers palette.

Note: For details about opening the Editor or opening palettes, see Chapter 1.

② Click one of the layers you want to link.

③ Press `Ctrl` and click one or more other layers that you want to link.

④ Click the **Link Layers** tool (⬚) in the Layers palette.

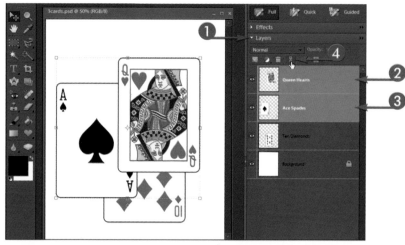

● A linking icon (⬚) appears next to each linked layer.

● To test that Photoshop Elements has linked the layers, select one of the layers, click the **Move** tool (⬚), and click and drag the layer.

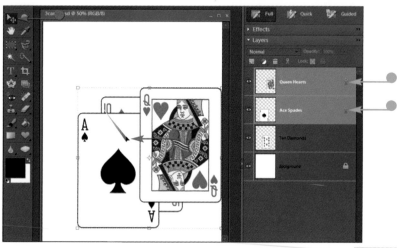

Merge Layers

Merging layers lets you permanently combine information from two or more separate layers. After merging layers, you can no longer move them independently of one another.

For more on moving a layer, see the section "Move a Layer."

Merge Layers

① In the Editor, display the Layers palette.

Note: *For details about opening the Editor or opening palettes, see Chapter 1.*

② Place the two layers you want to merge next to each other.

Note: *See the section "Reorder Layers" to change stacking order.*

③ Click the topmost of the two layers.

④ Click **Layer**.

⑤ Click **Merge Down**.

You can merge all the layers together by clicking **Flatten Image** or just the visible layers by clicking **Merge Visible**.

● The two layers merge.

Photoshop Elements keeps the name of the lower layer.

In this example, the Ace Spades layer has merged with the Queen Hearts layer.

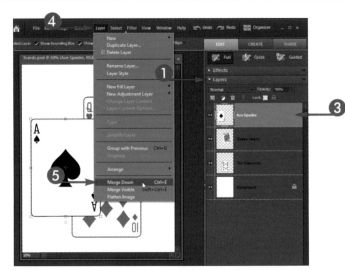

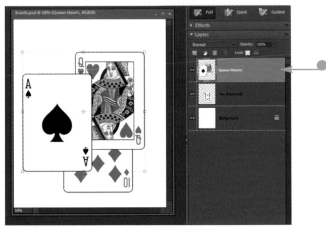

Rename
a Layer

You can rename a layer to give it a name that describes its content.

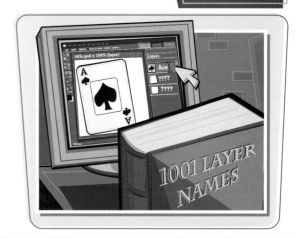

Rename a Layer

1. In the Editor, display the Layers palette.

Note: For details about opening the Editor or opening palettes, see Chapter 1.

2. Click a layer.

3. Click **Layer**.

4. Click **Rename Layer**.

The Layer Properties dialog box appears.

5. Type a new name for the layer.

6. Click **OK**.

● The name of the layer changes in the Layers palette.

You can also double-click the name of the layer in the Layers palette to edit the name in place.

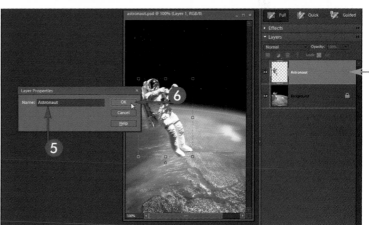

You can create a solid fill layer to place an opaque layer of color throughout your image. You can use fill layers behind layers containing objects to create all kinds of color effects in your photos.

Create a Fill Layer

① In the Editor, display the Layers palette.

Note: For details about opening the Editor or opening palettes, see Chapter 1.

② Click the layer you want to appear below the solid color layer.

③ Click **Layer**.

④ Click **New Fill Layer**.

⑤ Click **Solid Color**.

You can also create a gradient or pattern fill layer by clicking **Layer**, **New Fill Layer**, and then either **Gradient** or **Pattern**.

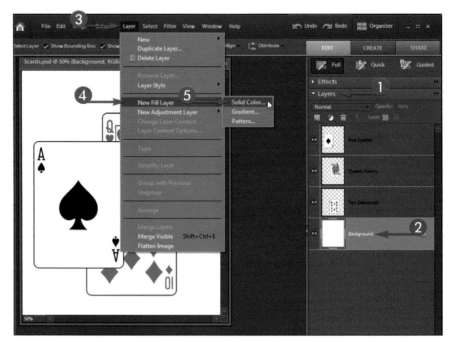

The New Layer dialog box appears.

⑥ Type a name for the layer, or use the default name.

● You can specify a type of blend or opacity setting for the layer.

Note: See the sections "Blend Layers" and "Change the Opacity of a Layer" for details.

⑦ Click **OK**.

The Color Picker dialog box appears.

8 To change the range of colors that appears in the window, click and drag the slider (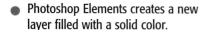).

9 To select a fill color, click in the color window.

10 Click **OK**.

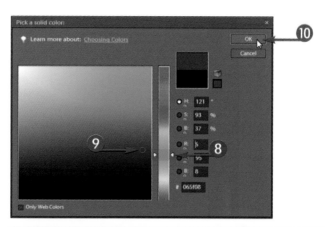

● Photoshop Elements creates a new layer filled with a solid color.

In this example, a solid green layer appears below the card layers.

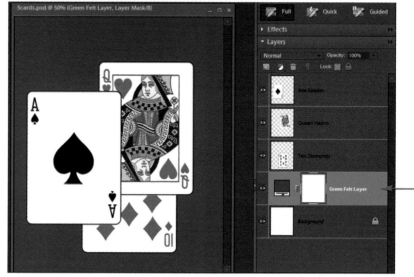

TIPS

How do I add solid color to just part of a layer?

To add color to a specific part of a layer, make a selection with a selection tool before creating the solid fill layer, then apply a color fill as outlined in the steps above. Photoshop Elements adds color only inside the selection.

What other types of fill layers can I add?

You can also create gradient fill layers, which apply bands of colors rather than a solid fill. Or you can create a pattern fill layer, which applies a repeating pattern as a fill instead of a solid color. You can select from a variety of preset gradient effects and patterns.

Create an Adjustment Layer

Adjustment layers let you store color and tonal changes in a layer instead of having them permanently applied to your image. The information in an adjustment layer is applied to the pixels in the layers below it.

You can use adjustment layers to test an editing technique without applying it to the original layer. Adjustment layers are especially handy for experimenting with colors, tones, and brightness settings.

Create an Adjustment Layer

① In the Editor, display the Layers palette.

Note: *For details about opening the Editor or opening palettes, see Chapter 1.*

② Click the layer you want to appear below the adjustment layer.

③ Click **Layer**.

④ Click **New Adjustment Layer**.

⑤ Click an adjustment command.

The New Layer dialog box appears.

⑥ Type a name for the adjustment layer, or use the default name.

● You can specify a type of blend or opacity setting for the layer.

Note: *See the sections "Blend Layers" and "Change the Opacity of a Layer" for details.*

⑦ Click **OK**.

● Photoshop Elements adds an adjustment layer to the image.

The dialog box for the adjustment command appears.

Note: *Depending on the type of adjustment layer you create, different settings appear.*

In this example, an adjustment layer is created that changes the hue and saturation.

⑧ Click and drag the sliders (■), or type values to adjust the settings.

You can see the adjustments take effect in the workspace.

⑨ Click **OK**.

● Photoshop Elements applies the effect to the layers that are below the adjustment layer.

You can double-click the adjustment layer to make changes to the settings.

TIPS

How do I apply an adjustment layer to only part of my image canvas?

Make a selection with a selection tool before creating the adjustment layer. Photoshop Elements turns the selected area into an adjustment layer. You can experiment with edits to the adjustment layer; any changes you make to the selection will affect the underlying layers. See Chapter 5 for more on the kinds of selections you can make with Elements' selection tools.

Is there a shortcut for creating an adjustment layer?

Yes. You can click the **Create Adjustment Layer** button (■) in the Layers palette and then click the type of adjustment layer you want to create.

Blend Layers

You can use Photoshop Elements' blending modes to specify how pixels in a layer should blend with the layers below. You can blend layers to create all kinds of visual effects in your photos.

In the following example, two photos are combined in one image file as two separate layers, and then the layers are blended together. To copy a photo into a layer, see the section "Create and Add to a Layer."

Blend Layers

BLEND A REGULAR LAYER

① In the Editor, display the Layers palette.

Note: For details about opening the Editor or opening palettes, see Chapter 1.

② Click the layer that you want to blend.

③ Click here and then click a blend mode.

Photoshop Elements blends the selected layer with the layers below it.

This example blends a sunset image with the image of a woman by using the Hard Light mode.

BLEND AN ADJUSTMENT LAYER

① Display the Layers palette.

② Click an adjustment layer that you want to blend.

③ Click here and then click a blend mode.

Photoshop Elements blends the selected layer with the layers below it.

This example shows the Exclusion mode applied to a Hue and Saturation adjustment layer, which creates a photonegative effect where the layers overlap.

TIPS

What effects do some of the different blending modes have?

The Multiply mode darkens the colors where the selected layer overlaps layers below it. The Screen mode is the opposite of Multiply; it lightens colors where layers overlap. Color takes the selected layer's colors and blends them with the details in the layers below it. Luminosity is the opposite of Color; it takes the selected layer's details and mixes them with the colors below it.

How do I copy and paste a selection from another photo?

Open the photo from which you want to copy, and select the item. You can press Ctrl + A to select everything, or you can press Ctrl + C to copy the selected area. Return to the photo to which you want to paste, click to select the layer you want to hold the pasted item, and then press Ctrl + A. If you do not select a layer prior to pasting, Elements creates a new layer.

Retouching Photos

Do you need to fix a photo fast? This chapter offers you all kinds of quick techniques for making simple retouches to your digital photos.

Retouch with Guided Edit

You can remove small blemishes and unwanted objects using the step-by-step instructions and adjustments in Elements' Guided Edit panel. The feature lets you compare before-and-after versions of an image as you retouch it.

Retouch with Guided Edit

① In the Editor, click **Guided**.

Note: For details about opening the Editor, see Chapter 1.

The Guided Edit panel opens.

● Make sure the Guided Activities list is open. You can click to open it (▶ changes to ▼).

② Click **Touch Up Scratches, Blemishes or Tear Marks**.

③ Click the **Spot Healing Brush** (🖌).

④ Click and drag the slider (◻) to select a brush size between 1 and 500.

Select a brush size that will cover the area you plan to touch up.

⑤ Click an object in your image.

Elements replaces the object with nearby pixels.

6 Click the **Healing Brush** (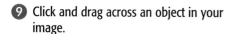).

7 Click and drag the slider (□) to select a brush size between 1 and 2500.

Select a brush size that is slightly smaller than the area you plan to touch up.

8 Press Alt and click an unblemished area of your image.

9 Click and drag across an object in your image.

Elements covers the object with pixels from the unblemished area.

TIP

When retouching in Guided Edit, how can I accurately view the objects I want to remove?

Guided Edit offers you a Zoom tool and Hand tool for adjusting your image and locating objects.

1 Click the **Zoom** tool (🔍).

2 Click inside your image to zoom in.

3 Click the **Hand** tool (✋).

4 Click and drag to move your image horizontally and vertically.

Note: For more about the Zoom and Hand tools, see Chapter 4.

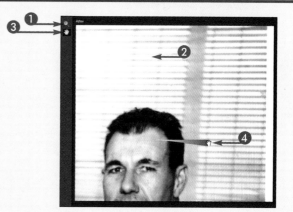

Quick Fix a Photo

Photoshop Elements' Quick Fix feature lets you make fast corrections to your photos in one convenient panel. You can adjust lighting, contrast, color, and focus and compare before-and-after views of your adjustments.

The Quick Fix interface consists of four palettes. The General Fixes palette includes Red Eye Fix and Smart Fix, which automatically corrects lighting, color, and contrast. The Lighting palette lets you fix contrast and exposure problems; the Color palette lets you fix color problems; and the Sharpen palette lets you sharpen photos.

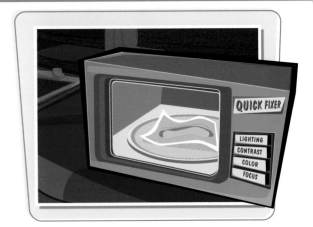

Quick Fix a Photo

① In the Editor, click **Quick**.

Note: For details about opening the Editor, see Chapter 1.

The Quick Fix panel opens.

● You can crop the image or fix a red-eye problem with these tools.

② Click here and then click a view mode.

The **After Only** view shows the results of your changes.

The **Before Only** view shows the original unedited photo.

The **Before and After** view shows both the original image and the image with changes applied.

③ Drag the Smart Fix slider (🔘).

● You can also click **Auto** to have Elements automatically adjust your image.

● Elements makes immediate adjustments to the lighting, contrast, and colors in the image.

● You can click **Reset** to return to the original settings.

● To adjust individual categories, click **Auto** for the type of correction you want to make.

● You can also drag a slider (🔘) to adjust the setting.

● In this example, the shadows in the image are lightened.

④ Click **Full**.

Photoshop Elements applies the changes and returns to the Full Edit panel.

Note: If you do not like the result of a Quick Fix, you can click Edit and then click Undo.

TIPS

Must I always use the Quick Fix feature to correct brightness, color, focus, and rotation problems?

No. You can make these corrections using other tools in Photoshop Elements. The Enhance menu contains these same corrections, some of which open dialog boxes that enable you to fine-tune the adjustment.

What exactly does the Smart Fix feature do?

Smart Fix analyzes your image and attempts to correct lighting, contrast, and color based on preset algorithms. Depending on the condition of the photo, the changes may be quite pronounced or barely noticeable. You can drag the Smart Fix slider (🔘) in the General Fixes palette to control the amount of change made to the color, shadows, and highlights in the image.

Remove Red Eye

You can use the Red Eye Removal tool to remove the red eye color that a camera flash can cause. Red eye is a common problem in snapshots taken indoors with a flash. The light from the flash reflects off the back of the subject's eyes, creating the red-eye appearance. Using the Red Eye Removal tool, you can edit the eye to change its color without changing image details.

Remove Red Eye

1 In the Editor, click the **Red Eye Removal** tool (🖸).

Note: For details about opening the Editor, see Chapter 1.

2 Click here and then drag the slider (🔲) to control the size of the area to correct.

Note: You can also fix red-eye problems in the Quick Fix window. See the section "Quick Fix a Photo" to learn more.

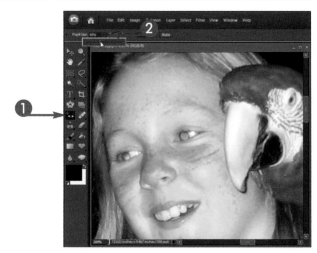

3 Click here and then drag the slider (🔲) to the darkness setting you want.

4 Click and drag over the eye you want to fix.

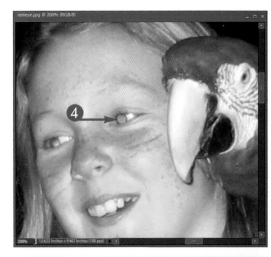

5 Release the mouse button.

Photoshop Elements repairs the color.

TIP

My pet photos have a green-eye problem. How do I fix this?

1 Click the **Burn** tool (⬤).

2 Set your brush style and size options.

3 Select **Highlights** in the Range menu.

4 Click an area you want to darken.

Photoshop Elements darkens the area.

You can click as many times as needed to darken the eye area.

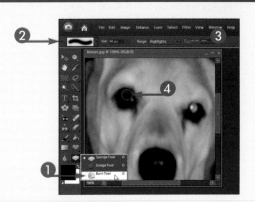

You can clean up small flaws or erase elements in your image with the Clone Stamp tool. The tool copies information from one area of an image to another. For example, you can use the Clone Stamp tool to remove unwanted blemishes of all kinds by cloning an area near the flaw and then stamping over the flaw.

Retouch with the Clone Stamp Tool

1 In the Editor, click the **Clone Stamp** tool ().

Note: *For details about opening the Editor, see Chapter 1.*

2 Click here and then select a brush size and type.

● You can also set an exact brush size here.

You can change the brush size while using the tool by pressing [and].

3 Press and hold Alt and click the area of the image from which you want to copy.

In this example, the Clone Stamp is used to remove a starfish from a beach.

④ Click or drag across the area of photo you want to correct.

Elements copies the cloned area to where you click and drag.

⑤ Continue clicking new areas to clone and dragging over the area as many times as needed to achieve the desired effect.

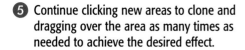

TIPS

How can I make the Clone Stamp's effects look seamless?

To erase elements from your image with the Clone Stamp without leaving a trace, try the following:

● Clone between areas of similar color and texture.

● To apply the stamp more subtly, lower its opacity.

● Use a soft-edged brush shape.

What can I do with the Pattern Stamp?

You can use the Pattern Stamp, which shares space in the toolbox with the Clone Stamp, to paint repeating patterns on your images. To find the Pattern Stamp tool, click and hold the **Clone Stamp** tool (🖊), and then click **Pattern Stamp** (🖊) from the menu that appears. You can then select a pattern, brush style, and brush size and stamp the pattern on your photo.

You can use the Spot Healing Brush to quickly repair flaws in a photo. The tool works well on small spots or blemishes on textured backgrounds.

The tool's Proximity Match setting analyzes pixels surrounding the selected area and replaces the area with a patch of similar pixels. The Create Texture setting replaces the area with a blend of surrounding pixels.

Correct a Spot

① In the Editor, click the **Spot Healing Brush** tool ().

Note: For details about opening the Editor, see Chapter 1.

② Click here and then select a brush size and type.

● You can also set an exact brush size here.

③ Click here and select the type of healing effect you want to apply (● changes to ○).

Proximity Match applies pixels from around the selected area.

Create Texture applies a blend of pixels from the selected area.

④ Click the spot you want to correct.

● Elements replaces the selected area with pixels similar to those nearby.

TIP

How do I correct larger areas of a photo?
Using the Healing Brush tool, follow these steps:

① Click and hold the **Spot Healing Brush** tool (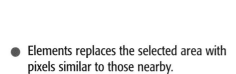).

② Click **Healing Brush Tool** (✐).

③ Adjust the tool's settings.

④ Press and hold Alt and click the area you want to clone.

⑤ Drag over the problem area to blend the colored pixels into the new area.

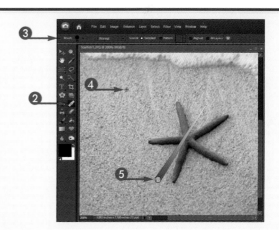

Remove Dust and Scratches

You can add subtle blurring to your image to remove extraneous dust and scratches with the Dust & Scratches filter. This can help improve scans of old photographs.

Remove Dust and Scratches

① In the Editor, select the layer to which you want to apply the filter.

Note: *For details about opening the Editor, see Chapter 1.*

② Use a selection tool to select an area that has dust and scratches.

Note: *For more about layers, see Chapter 7. For more on using the selection tools, see Chapter 5.*

③ Click **Filter**.

④ Click **Noise**.

⑤ Click **Dust & Scratches**.

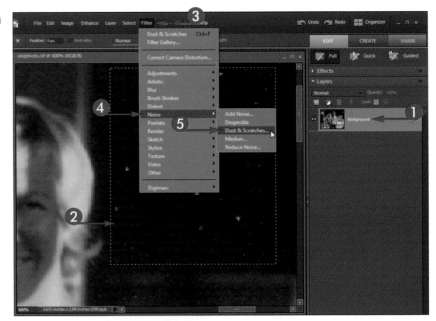

The Dust & Scratches dialog box appears.

● Photoshop Elements displays a small preview of the effect.

⑥ Click and drag the Radius slider (▣) to control what size speck Elements considers dust or a scratch.

⑦ Click and drag the Threshold slider to specify how much the pixels must differ from their surroundings to be considered dust or a scratch.

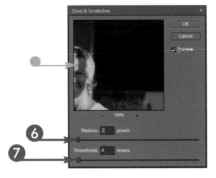

● In this example, the Threshold value has been increased slightly to avoid blurring.

⑧ Click **OK**.

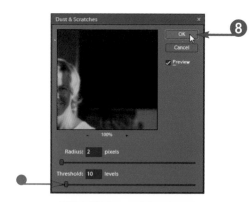

● Photoshop Elements applies the filter.

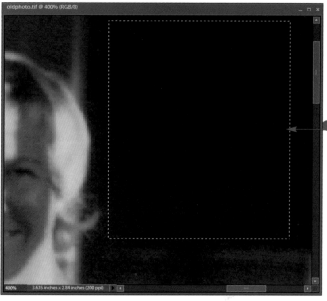

What does the Dust & Scratches filter do to areas of an image that do not have dust or scratches?

Although the intention of the Dust & Scratches filter is to remove only minor artifacts from an image, it still adds some blur wherever you apply it. For this reason, selecting areas that have dust and scratches before applying the filter is best. This prevents the filter from affecting details in an image unnecessarily.

How do I adjust the preview in the Dust & Scratches dialog box?

You can click minus (−) or plus (+) below the preview area to change the preview window's magnification setting. You can also position the mouse pointer over the preview area and drag your view of the image to another area of the photo.

Crop an Image

The Crop tool lets you quickly change the size of an image to remove unneeded space on the sides. Cropping is also a great way to edit out unwanted background elements in a photo or reposition a subject in your photo.

Another way to crop an image is by changing its canvas size. See Chapter 4 for more information about setting a new canvas size. Yet another way is by selecting an area with a selection tool, clicking Image, and then clicking Crop. See Chapter 5 for more about making selections.

Crop an Image

① In the Editor, click the **Crop** tool (▱).

Note: For details about opening the Editor, see Chapter 1.

② Click and drag to select the area of the image you want to keep.

Another way to crop an image is by changing its canvas size; you do this by clicking **Image**, **Resize**, and **Canvas Size**, and then typing new dimensions for the image.

● You can set specific dimensions for a crop using the Width and Height boxes in the Options bar.

③ Click and drag the side and corner handles (▢) to adjust the size of the cropping boundary.

You can click and drag inside the cropping boundary to move it without adjusting its size.

④ Click ✅ or press `Enter` to commit your changes.

You can also double-click inside the crop area to crop the photo.

● To exit the cropping process, you can click ⊘ or press `Esc` to cancel.

Photoshop Elements crops the image, deleting the pixels outside the cropping boundary.

Note: *You can also crop images in the Quick Fix window. See the section "Quick Fix a Photo" to learn more about this window.*

TIP

How do I move my cropping area?

① Position the mouse pointer inside the crop area (⬚ changes to ▶).

② Click and drag the crop area to the portion of the image you want to crop.

● You can click and drag the handles (⬚) to adjust the cropping dimensions.

③ Click ✅ or press `Enter` to complete the crop.

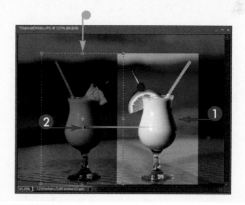

Crop with the Cookie Cutter Tool

You can use the Cookie Cutter tool to crop your photos into shapes. This tool is similar to the standard Crop tool, which lets you crop your photos into rectangular shapes.

The Cookie Cutter tool is handy when you want to crop a photo into a shape and display it over a solid color. See Chapter 7 for more on creating a solid-color fill layer.

Crop with the Cookie Cutter Tool

1 In the Editor, click the layer to which you want to apply the crop.

Note: *For details about opening the Editor, see Chapter 1.*

2 Click the **Cookie Cutter** tool ().

3 Click here and then click a shape for the crop.

● You can click here to change the crop shape.

● The Unconstrained option, which is the default setting, allows you to draw a freeform shape for the crop.

④ Click and drag to create the shape on the image.

Photoshop Elements crops the shape, and any areas outside the shape reveal the underlying layer.

● In this example, the underlying layer is a fill layer.

Click ☑ or press Enter to commit your changes.

Photoshop Elements applies the cropping effect.

TIP

How can I remove the extra space around the cookie-cutter shape?

You can select the **Crop** option to have the tool remove the extra space around the applied shape:

① Follow steps **1** to **3** in this task.

② Click to select **Crop** in the Options bar (■ changes to ☑).

③ Click and drag to create the shape on the image.

④ Click ☑ or press Enter to commit your changes.

Photoshop Elements crops as it applies the tool.

Rotate an Image

You can rotate an image to turn it within the image canvas, or to flip it horizontally or vertically. If you import or scan a horizontal image vertically, you can rotate it so that it appears in the correct orientation.

You can also flip a photo to change the direction of the subject matter. Flipping it horizontally, for example, creates a mirror image of the photo.

Rotate an Image

1 In the Editor, click **Image**.

Note: For details about opening the Editor, see Chapter 1.

2 Click **Rotate**.

3 Click **90° Left** or **90° Right** to rotate an image.

● To flip an image on an axis, select **Flip Horizontal** or **Flip Vertical**.

Photoshop Elements rotates the image.

Straighten an Image

You can easily straighten an image that was scanned in crookedly.

Straighten an Image

① In the Editor, click **Image**.

Note: For details about opening the Editor, see Chapter 1.

② Click **Rotate**.

③ Click **Straighten Image**.

Photoshop Elements straightens the image.

You may need to crop the image to compensate for white edges created by the scan or any transparent edges created by the straightening effect.

Note: See the section "Crop an Image" for more on cropping features.

Sharpen an Image

You can use the Unsharp Mask command to sharpen an image suffering from focus problems. The Unsharp Mask dialog box lets you control the amount of sharpening you apply.

To apply the enhancement to just part of your image, you can select that part with a selection tool. To use the selection tools, see Chapter 5.

Sharpen an Image

① In the Editor, select the layer you want to sharpen.

Note: For details about opening the Editor, see Chapter 1. For more about layers, see Chapter 7.

In this example, the image has a single Background layer.

② Click **Enhance**.

③ Click **Unsharp Mask**.

The Unsharp Mask dialog box appears.

● A small window displays a preview of the filter's effect.

● You can click here to preview the effect in the main window (■ changes to ✔).

④ Click minus or plus (− or +) to zoom out or in.

⑤ Click and drag the sliders (▣) to control the amount of sharpening you apply to the image.

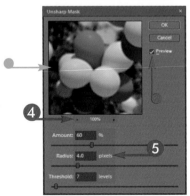

● **Amount** controls the overall amount of sharpening.

● **Radius** controls whether sharpening is confined to edges in the image (low Radius setting) or added across the entire image (high Radius setting).

● **Threshold** controls how much contrast must be present for an edge to be recognized and sharpened.

⑥ Click **OK**.

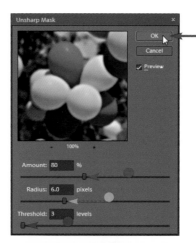

Photoshop Elements applies the sharpening.

TIPS

When should I apply sharpening?
Sharpening an image after you change its size is a good idea because changing an image's size can add blurring. Applying the Unsharp Mask enhancement can also help clarify scanned images. Although the Unsharp Mask enhancement cannot perform a miracle and make an unfocused image completely clear, it can sharpen up slightly blurred images or blurring caused by applying other filters.

Is the Auto Sharpen button in the Quick Fix window the same as Unsharp Mask?
Yes. The Auto button on the Sharpen palette sharpens an image by a preset amount. If you use the Quick Fix window to retouch a photo, you can easily apply the Auto Sharpen command. However, you can fine-tune the sharpening effects to your liking when using the Unsharp Mask dialog box.

Extract an Object from a Background

You can extract an object in your photo from its background using the Magic Extractor tool. You define the object and background by brushing lines over them, and then Elements deletes the background automatically.

Using the Magic Extractor can be quicker than selecting the object with one of the Lasso tools, inverting the selection, and then deleting the background. For more information about the Lasso tools, see Chapter 5.

Extract an Object from a Background

① In the Editor, click **Image**.

Note: For details about opening the Editor, see Chapter 1.

② Click **Magic Extractor**.

The Magic Extractor dialog box opens.

③ Click the **Foreground Brush** tool (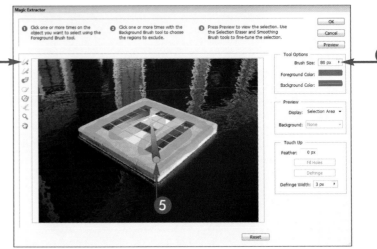).

④ Click here to specify your brush size.

⑤ Click and drag to apply brush strokes to the object you want to keep.

The more of the object you cover, the greater the chance of a successful extraction.

6. Click the **Background Brush** tool (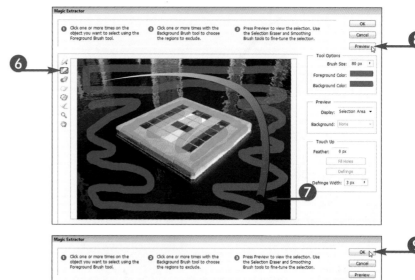).

7. Click and drag to apply brush lines on the background you want to remove.

8. Click **Preview**.

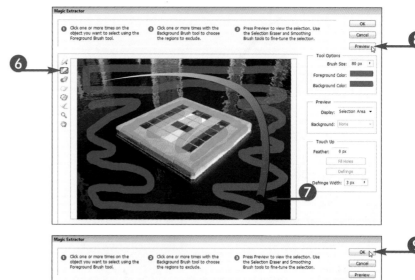

Elements extracts the object from the background and displays a preview.

To repeat the process, press and hold **Alt** to change Cancel to Reset and then click **Reset**.

9. Click **OK** to complete the extraction and return to your image.

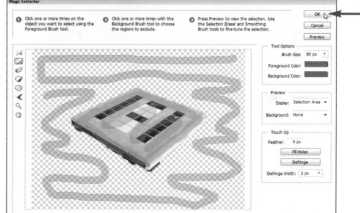

TIP

How can I clean up the edges of an object after extraction?

While still in the Magic Extractor dialog box, you can remove unwanted pixels from the edges of your object with the Remove From Selection tool. Follow these steps:

1. Use the Magic Extractor to preview your extraction.

2. Use the **Zoom** (🔍) and **Hand** (✋) tools to view the edge of the object.

3. Click the **Remove From Selection** (🖌️) tool.

4. Click and drag to clean up the edges of the object.

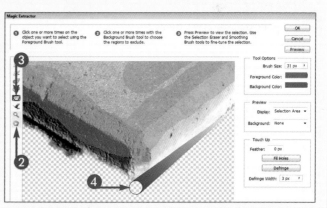

Enhancing Contrast and Exposure

Does your photo suffer from shadows that are too dark or highlights that are too light? Or perhaps you have an old photo in which the entire image is faded. You can correct tone, contrast, exposure, and lighting problems using several nifty tools in Photoshop Elements. This chapter shows you how.

Enhance Lighting with Guided Edit

You can fix simple lighting problems in your images using the step-by-step instructions and adjustments in Elements' Guided Edit panel. The feature lets you compare before-and-after versions of an image as you change the lighting.

1 In the Editor, click **Guided**.

Note: *For details about opening the Editor, see Chapter 1.*

The Guided Edit panel opens.

● Make sure the Lighting and Exposure list is open. You can click here to open it (▶ changes to ▼).

2 Click **Lighten or Darken**.

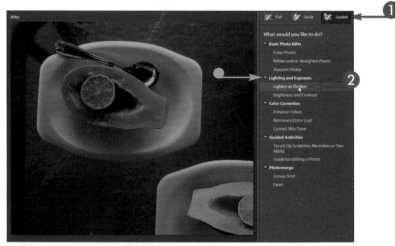

● You can click **Auto** to have Elements automatically adjust the lighting in your image using its built-in optimization routines.

3 Click the view button (▣) to open before-and-after views of the image (▣ changes to ▦).

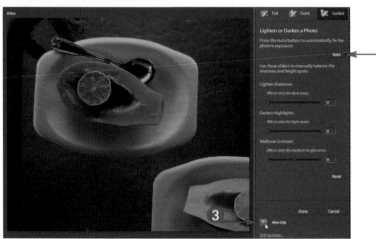

④ Click and drag the slider (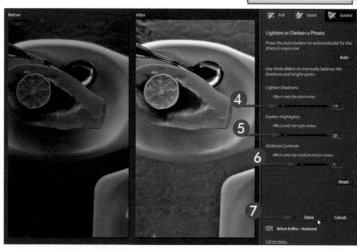) to lighten shadows in the image.

⑤ Click and drag the slider to darken highlights in the image.

⑥ Click and drag the slider to increase or decrease the contrast in the image.

⑦ Click **Done**.

Elements enhances the lighting in the image.

● You can click **Full** to switch to the Full Edit.

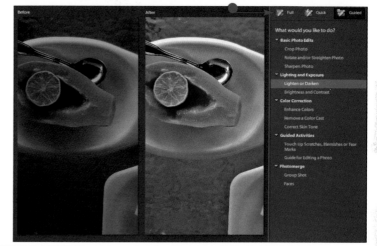

TIP

Is there a way to automatically adjust lighting and color in one step?

You can have Elements automatically optimize the light and color at the same time with the Smart Fix feature. The feature can be a good first step in trying to fix exposure problems.

① Click **Enhance**.

② Click **Adjust Smart Fix**.

The Adjust Smart Fix dialog box opens.

③ Click and drag the slider () to control the strength of the adjustment.

④ Click **OK**.

Elements applies the adjustment.

Adjust Levels

You can fine-tune shadows, highlights, and midtones in your image using the Levels dialog box. Input sliders enable you to manipulate the tonal qualities and color balance of an image, and the output sliders let you adjust contrast.

You can adjust levels in just a part of your image by making a selection or selecting a layer before executing the command. For more on making selections, see Chapter 5. For more on working with layers, see Chapter 7.

Adjust Levels

1. In the Editor, click **Enhance**.

Note: For details about opening the Editor, see Chapter 1.

2. Click **Adjust Lighting**.

3. Click **Levels**.

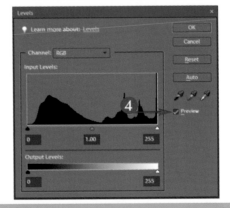

The Levels dialog box opens.

4. Make sure the **Preview** option is selected (■ changes to ✓).

The Preview option lets you see your adjustments as you make them.

5 Click and drag the slider (■) to the right to darken shadows and increase contrast.

6 Click and drag the slider (■) to adjust the midtones of the image.

7 Click and drag the slider (■) to lighten the bright areas of the image and increase contrast.

● Elements displays a preview of the adjustments in the workspace.

8 Click and drag the slider (■) to the right to lighten the image.

9 Click and drag the slider (■) to the left to darken the image.

10 Click **OK**.

Elements applies the adjustments.

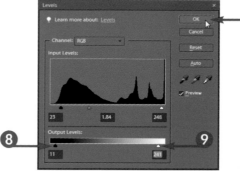

TIPS

How do I adjust the brightness levels of an image automatically?

Click **Enhance** and then **Auto Levels**. Elements sets the lightest pixels to white and the darkest pixels to black, and then redistributes the intermediate values proportionally throughout the rest of the image. You can use the Auto Levels command to make immediate corrections to shadows, midtones, and highlights.

Can I tell Elements which pixels to use as the darkest, midtone, and brightest levels in my image?

Yes. The Levels dialog box includes three Eyedropper tools, one each for the darkest (✐), midtone (✐), and lightest (✐) tones. You can click the Eyedropper tool for the tone you want to set and then click the appropriate pixel in your image.

Adjust Shadows and Highlights

You can use the Shadows and Highlights feature to make quick adjustments to the dark and light areas of your image. The feature is less complicated than the Levels tool, but also less flexible.

You can adjust shadows and highlights in just a part of your image by making a selection or selecting a layer before executing the command. For more on making selections, see Chapter 5. For more on working with layers, see Chapter 7.

Adjust Shadows and Highlights

① In the Editor, click **Enhance**.

Note: For details about opening the Editor, see Chapter 1.

② Click **Adjust Lighting**.

③ Click **Shadows/Highlights**.

The Shadows/Highlights dialog box opens.

④ Make sure the **Preview** option is selected (■ changes to ✓).

The Preview option lets you view your adjustments as you make them.

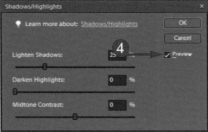

⑤ Click and drag the slider () to lighten shadows in the image.

⑥ Click and drag the slider to darken highlights in the image.

⑦ Click and drag the slider to adjust midtone contrast in the image.

⑧ Click **OK**.

Elements applies the adjustments.

How do I cancel my adjustments without exiting the Shadows/Highlights dialog box?

If you press and hold Alt, Cancel changes to Reset. Click **Reset** to return the dialog box to its original default settings.

When I open the Shadows/Highlights dialog box, Elements immediately adjusts my image. What is happening?

The Shadows/Highlights filter is set to automatically lighten shadows in your image by 25%. When you open the dialog box, you will see this applied. You can reduce the effect by dragging the Lighten Shadows slider (■) to the left.

Change Brightness and Contrast

You can use the Brightness/Contrast dialog box to adjust the brightness and contrast levels in a photo or a selected portion of a photo. *Brightness* refers to the intensity of the lighter pixels in an image, and *contrast* refers to the relative difference between dark and light areas in an image.

To make more complex adjustments to the tonal qualities in an image, use the Levels dialog box. See the section "Adjust Levels" for more information.

Change Brightness and Contrast

① In the Editor, click **Enhance**.

Note: For details about opening the Editor, see Chapter 1.

② Click **Adjust Lighting**.

③ Click **Brightness/Contrast**.

The Brightness/Contrast dialog box appears.

If you want to restrict changes to a selection or layer, select the layer or make the selection before executing the command.

● The Preview check box is selected by default.

④ Click and drag the Brightness slider (🔲) to adjust brightness.

Drag the slider to the right to lighten the image.

Drag the slider to the left to darken the image.

● You can also type a number from 1 to 100 to lighten the image or from –1 to –100 to darken the image.

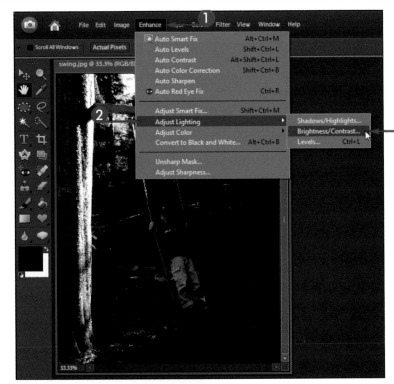

⑤ Click and drag the Contrast slider (█) to adjust contrast.

Drag the slider to the right to increase contrast.

Drag the slider to the left to decrease contrast.

● You can also type a number from 1 to 100 to increase contrast or from –1 to –100 to decrease contrast.

⑥ Click **OK**.

Elements applies the adjustments to the image, selection, or layer.

(TIPS)

How can I adjust the contrast of an image automatically?

You can click **Enhance** and then **Auto Contrast**. Elements automatically converts light and dark pixels for you. The Auto Contrast feature converts the very lightest pixels in the image to white and the very darkest pixels to black. Unlike with the Brightness/Contrast dialog box, you cannot fine-tune the contrast settings with Auto Contrast.

Does Elements offer a tool for evaluating tones in an image?

Yes. You can use the Histogram palette to evaluate tonal qualities in your images. Click **Window** and then **Histogram** to open the palette. The Histogram is a graphical representation of the light and dark pixels in your image, plotted by intensity. The density of each color intensity is plotted, with the darker pixels plotted on the left and the lighter pixels plotted on the right.

Lighten Areas with the Dodge Tool

You can use the Dodge tool to quickly brighten a specific area of an image. *Dodge* is a photographic term that describes the diffusing of light when developing a film negative. For example, you can tweak a dark area of an image by brushing over the area with the Dodge tool.

You can fine-tune the effects of the Dodge tool by specifying which tones to correct — midtones, shadows, or highlights. You can also specify the strength of the lightening effect by selecting an exposure setting.

Lighten Areas with the Dodge Tool

① In the Editor, click and hold the **Sponge** tool (🖐).

Note: For details about opening the Editor, see Chapter 1.

The Dodge tool shares space with the Sponge and Burn tools in the toolbox.

② Click **Dodge Tool** (🔍).

③ Click here and then click the brush you want to use.

● You can also select an exact brush size here.

You can change the brush size while using the tool by pressing ⬜ and ⬜.

- You can click here to select the range of tones you want to affect.

- You can click here to select the tool's exposure, or strength.

④ Click and drag the mouse pointer (○) over the area you want to lighten.

- Photoshop Elements lightens the area.

If you continue to click or click and drag over an area, the area is lightened more with each application of the tool.

Is there a way to gradually brighten an area?

If you set the Exposure level to a low value, you can drag repeatedly over the area you want to correct to gradually brighten the area. Or you can click multiple times to gradually brighten just the area under the cursor.

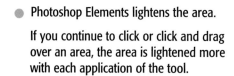

How can I add extra highlights to the lighter area of an object?

You can apply the Dodge tool with the Range set to Highlights to brighten the lighter areas of an object in your image. Likewise, you can use the Burn tool (⬛) with the Range set to Shadows to add shadows to the shaded side of an object. For more on the Burn tool, see the section "Darken Areas with the Burn Tool."

Darken Areas with the Burn Tool

You can use the Burn tool to darken a specific area of an image. *Burn* is a photographic term that describes the focusing of light when developing a film negative. For example, you can tweak a bright area of an image by brushing over the area with the Burn tool.

You can fine-tune the effects of the Burn tool by specifying which tones to correct — midtones, shadows, or highlights. You can also specify the strength of the darkening effect by selecting an exposure setting.

Darken Areas with the Burn Tool

① In the Editor, click and hold the **Sponge** tool (🟤).

Note: *For details about opening the Editor, see Chapter 1.*

The Burn tool shares space with the Sponge and Dodge tools in the toolbox.

② Click **Burn Tool** (🟤).

③ Click here and then click the brush you want to use.

● You can also select the range of colors you want to affect and the tool's exposure, or strength.

④ Click and drag the mouse pointer (○) over the area you want to darken.

Photoshop Elements darkens the area.

● If you continue to click or click and drag over an area, the area is darkened more with each application of the tool.

In this example, a shadow is cast against the cup.

How do I invert the bright and dark colors in an image?

You can apply the Invert filter to make the image look like a film negative. Bright colors become dark, and vice versa. To apply the Invert filter, follow these steps:

① Click **Filter**.

② Click **Adjustments**.

③ Click **Invert**.

Photoshop Elements inverts the image.

Note: For more on Photoshop Elements' filters, see Chapter 12.

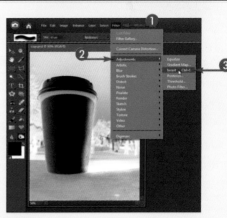

You can use Photoshop Elements' Lighting Effects filter to create the illusion of spotlights and directional lights in an image. Elements offers 17 light styles that can help add ambiance to your images. After you assign a light style, you can control the direction of the light source and the focus of the beam.

Omni lights shine directly over an object.
Spotlights create an elliptical beam of light.
Directional lights shine light from one angle.

Add a Spotlight

1 In the Editor, select the layer to which you want to apply the filter.

Note: For details about opening the Editor, see Chapter 1. For more about layers, see Chapter 7.

2 Click **Filter**.

3 Click **Render**.

4 Click **Lighting Effects**.

The Lighting Effects dialog box appears.

● Photoshop Elements displays a small preview of the effect.

5 Click here and then click a lighting style.

Note: Some light styles use multiple lights; you must position each light in the set and adjust the settings individually.

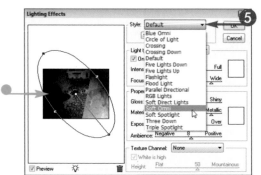

● Optionally, you can click here and click a light type.

⑥ Adjust the position and shape of the lighting by clicking and dragging the handles in the preview window.

● You can click and drag the center point to change where the light is centered.

⑦ Click and drag the Intensity slider (▣) to control the light intensity.

⑧ Click **OK**.

Photoshop Elements applies the filter.

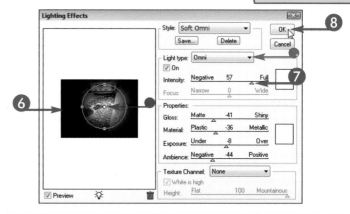

TIP

What is lens flare, and how can I add it to an image?
Lens flare is the extra flash of light that sometimes appears in a photo when too much light enters the camera lens.

① Click **Filter**.

② Click **Render**.

③ Click **Lens Flare**.

④ In the Lens Flare dialog box, drag the slider (▣) to control the brightness.

⑤ Drag the mouse pointer (+) to position the lens flare in your image.

⑥ Click **OK**.

● Photoshop Elements adds the lens flare effect.

Fix an Underexposed Image

You can use blending modes and layers to improve the lighting in underexposed images. The Multiply blending mode creates intense, dark colors, and the Screen mode lightens colors by blending them. By combining the two modes, you can modify the light in an image.

You use blending modes with Levels Adjustment layers to fine-tune the light and dark tones in an underexposed image. You may need to experiment with the number of layers and blending modes to achieve the right effect for your particular image.

Fix an Underexposed Image

1 In the Editor, add three Levels Adjustment layers to the Layers palette.

Note: For details about opening the Editor, see Chapter 1. For more about layers, see Chapter 7.

Note: Your own photo may require more or fewer Adjustment layers and blending modes to achieve the look you want.

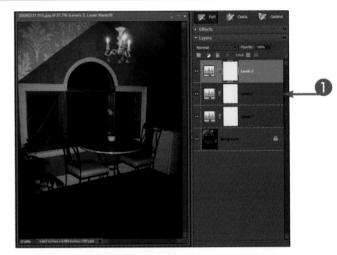

2 Click the first Adjustment layer.

3 Click here and then click **Multiply**.

The Multiply blending mode multiplies the image's base colors, resulting in darker, more intense colors.

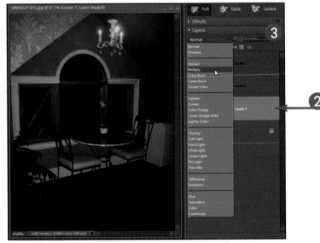

④ Click the second Adjustment layer.

⑤ Click here and then click **Screen**.

The Screen blending mode produces a lighter overall color by blending the layers and emphasizing the lighter pixels.

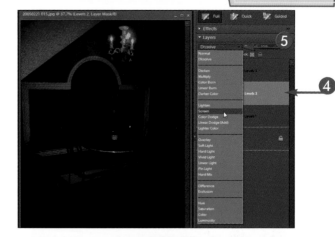

⑥ Double-click the third Adjustment layer's Levels thumbnail.

The Levels dialog box opens.

⑦ Drag the Highlights slider (△) and Midtones slider (△) to the left to lighten the image.

⑧ Click **OK**.

Photoshop Elements applies the adjustments.

Note: You may need to tweak the settings to create the desired effect for your photo.

 TIPS

Can I use the Brightness/Contrast command to fix an exposure problem?

Although the name implies that it may improve brightness issues, the Brightness/Contrast filter does not necessarily correct overly light or overly dark images. Boosting brightness values in an image makes all the image's pixels lighter, while lowering the values makes all the pixels darker. For most photos, you do not need to adjust all the pixels — just those affected by the exposure problem. See the section "Change Brightness and Contrast" for more about the Brightness/Contrast command.

How do I fix an overexposed photo?

Depending on the amount of overexposure, you can use the Levels dialog box to make adjustments to the midtones, shadows, and highlights in your photo. By subtracting light from the image, you can make subtle corrections to an overexposed snapshot. See the section "Adjust Levels" for more information.

Using the Blur and Sharpen Tools

You can sharpen or blur specific areas of your image with the Blur and Sharpen tools. This allows you to emphasize or de-emphasize objects in a photo. You can use the Blur tool to make tiny specks and other small flaws less noticeable in your photos. You can use the Sharpen tool to sharpen the edges of an object.

You can blur or sharpen the entire image by using one of the Blur filters or the Unsharp Mask. See Chapter 8 to sharpen an image, and Chapter 12 for more information on filters.

USING THE BLUR TOOL

① In the Editor, click the **Blur** tool (![icon]).

Note: For details about opening the Editor, see Chapter 1.

The Blur tool shares space in the toolbox with the Sharpen and Smudge tools.

② Click here and then click the brush you want to use.

● To change the strength of the tool, type a value from 1% to 100%.

③ Click and drag the mouse pointer (○) to blur an area of the image.

Photoshop Elements blurs the area.

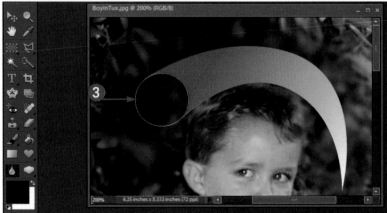

USING THE SHARPEN TOOL

1 Click and hold the **Blur** tool ().

2 Click **Sharpen Tool** (▲).

The Sharpen tool shares space in the toolbox with the Blur and Smudge tools.

3 Click here and then click the brush you want to use.

● To change the strength of the tool, type a value from 1% to 100%.

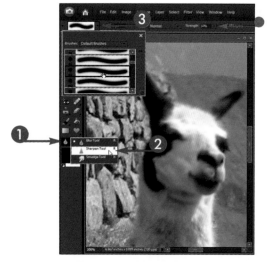

4 Click and drag the mouse pointer (○) to sharpen an area of the image.

Photoshop Elements sharpens the area.

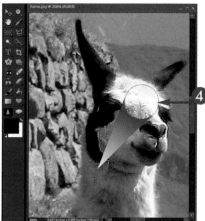

TIPS

What is the Smudge tool?
The Smudge tool (☞) is another tool you can use to create interesting blur effects in your photos. It simulates dragging a finger through wet paint, shifting and smearing colors in your image. The Smudge tool shares space in the toolbox with the Blur and Sharpen tools.

Is there a filter I can use to sharpen or blur an entire image?
Yes. Photoshop Elements includes a sharpening feature, called Unsharp Mask, that you can use to sharpen the appearance of pixels in a photo. For more on sharpening an image, see Chapter 8. You can also select from several blurring filters, including Gaussian Blur, to make your image appear blurry. For more on blurring an image, see Chapter 12.

Enhancing Colors

Do your photos suffer from faded colors or unattractive color casts? This chapter shows you how to use the tools in Photoshop Elements to correct color problems in your images by adding, removing, or shifting colors.

Posterized

Enhance Colors with Guided Edit

You can enhance or shift the colors in your images using the step-by-step instructions and adjustments in Elements' Guided Edit panel. The panel lets you compare before-and-after versions of an image as you adjust the colors.

Enhance Colors with Guided Edit

1. In the Editor, click **Guided**.

Note: For details about opening the Editor, see Chapter 1.

   The Guided Edit panel opens.

● Make sure the Color Correction list is open. You can click here to open it (▶ changes to ▼).

2. Click **Enhance Colors**.

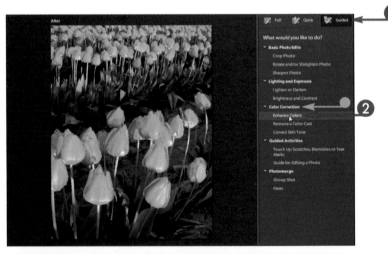

● You can click **Auto** to have Elements automatically balance the colors and contrast using its built-in optimization routines.

3. Click the **View** button (▤) to open before-and-after views of the image (▤ changes to ▥).

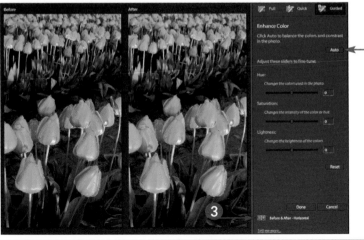

194

④ Click and drag the Hue slider (▣) to shift the colors in the image.

⑤ Click and drag the Saturation slider to change the color intensity in the image.

⑥ Click and drag the Lightness slider to change the lightness of the colors in the image.

⑦ Click **Done**.

Elements adjusts the colors in the image.

● You can click **Full** to switch to the Full Edit interface.

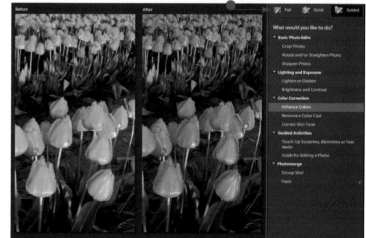

TIP

How can I limit my color adjustments to one type of color in my image?

The Hue/Saturation dialog box lets you make some of the same color adjustments as in Guided Edit. It also lets you limit the adjustments to a specific type of color:

① Click **Enhance**.

② Click **Adjust Color**.

③ Click **Adjust Hue/Saturation**.

④ Click here and select a color type.

⑤ Click the sliders (▣) to make adjustments.

⑥ Click **OK**.

Photoshop Elements adjusts the color.

Adjust Skin Color

You can improve skin colors that appear tinted or washed out in your images. After you sample an area of skin with the eyedropper, Elements adjusts the skin color to make it look more natural. Elements also adjusts other colors in the image based on the sampled skin.

Adjust Skin Color

① In the Editor, click **Enhance**.

Note: For details about opening the Editor, see Chapter 1.

② Click **Adjust Color**.

③ Click **Adjust Color for Skin Tone**.

The Adjust Color for Skin Tone dialog box appears.

● The mouse pointer (🖑) changes to an eyedropper (🖊️).

④ Click an area of skin in your image.

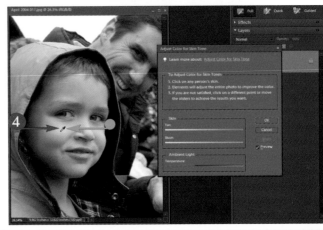

Elements adjusts the skin tones and other colors in your image.

⑤ Click and drag the Tan slider (▣) to adjust the level of brown in the skin tones.

⑥ Click and drag the Blush slider to adjust the level of red in the skin tones.

⑦ Click and drag the Temperature slider to adjust the overall coloring of the skin tones.

⑧ Click **OK**.

Photoshop Elements makes adjustments to the skin in the image.

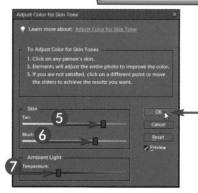

TIP

Can I have Photoshop Elements correct all the colors in my image automatically?

The Auto Color Correction command adjusts the photo based on the mix of highlights, midtones, and shadows in the image. It maps the darkest and lightest pixels based on a default set of values and neutralizes the midtones. Follow these steps to apply the command:

① Click the layer you want to adjust.

② Click **Enhance**.

③ Click **Auto Color Correction**.

Photoshop Elements adjusts the image colors.

Adjust Color with the Sponge Tool

You can use the Sponge tool to make simple adjustments to the color saturation or color intensity of a specific area of an image. For example, you may want to make a person's clothing appear more colorful or tone down an element that is too colorful.

Adjust Color with the Sponge Tool

DECREASE SATURATION

1 In the Editor, click the **Sponge** tool ().

Note: For details about opening the Editor, see Chapter 1.

The Sponge tool shares space with the Dodge and Burn tools in the toolbox. You may need to press and hold a tool and then select it from the menu.

2 Click the brush style you want to use.

● You can also click here and drag the slider (▣) that appears to set a brush size.

3 Click here and then select **Desaturate**.

4 Click and drag the mouse pointer (○) to decrease the saturation of an area of the image.

In this example, a section of the tulip field is desaturated.

To confine the effect to a particular area, you can make a selection prior to applying the tool. See Chapter 5 for more about making selections.

INCREASE SATURATION

① Perform steps **1** and **2** on the previous page.

② Click here and then select **Saturate**.

③ Click and drag the mouse pointer (○) to increase the saturation of an area of the image.

● You can adjust the strength of the Sponge tool by clicking here and moving the slider (▣) between 1% and 100%.

In this example, the colors of an ice cream cone are intensified.

To confine the effect to a particular area, you can make a selection prior to applying the tool. See Chapter 5 for more about making selections.

TIPS

What does the Flow setting do?

Clicking the Flow drop-down arrow (▾) in the Options bar displays a Flow slider (▣) that you can use to control the intensity of the saturation. You can set the Flow anywhere from 1% to 100% to determine how much the sponge saturates or desaturates the pixels in your image. Start with the 50% Flow setting and then experiment with increasing or decreasing the percentage to get the amount of control you want.

How do I find the right brush style and size?

The Brushes palette displays a variety of brush styles with soft, hard, and shaped edges. To blend your sponging effect into the surrounding pixels, select a soft-edge brush style. To make your sponging effect appear more distinct, use a hard-edge brush style. Shaped edges can help you produce textured effects. Clicking the Size drop-down arrow (▾) in the Options bar lets you modify the brush size. You can also press [or] while sponging to change your brush size. To check how your brush size compares to your image, move the Sponge tool over the image window without clicking.

Correct Color with Color Variations

You can use the Color Variations feature to quickly fix color casts and other color problems in a photo. Color casts result from unfavorable lighting conditions. For example, when you shoot a subject under fluorescent lights, your photograph may take on a greenish color. Age can also add casts to a photo.

If you make a selection before performing the Color Variations command, you affect only the selected pixels. Similarly, if you have a multilayered image, your adjustments affect only the selected layer. See Chapter 5 for more on making a selection and Chapter 7 for more on layers.

Correct Color with Color Variations

1 In the Editor, click **Enhance**.

Note: For details about opening the Editor, see Chapter 1.

2 Click **Adjust Color**.

3 Click **Color Variations**.

Note: See Chapter 7 to read more about layers.

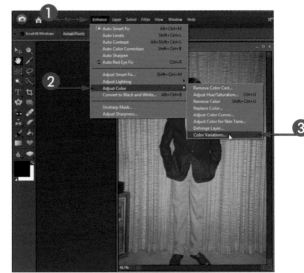

The Color Variations dialog box appears.

4 Select a tonal range to apply effects to the different tones of your image (● changes to ○).

● Alternatively, you can click to select **Saturation** (● changes to ○).

5 Click and drag the slider (▣) left to make small adjustments or right to make large adjustments.

6 To add or subtract a color, click one of the thumbnails.

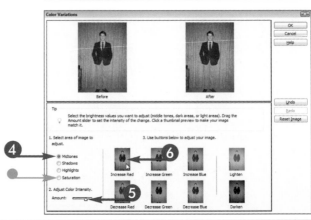

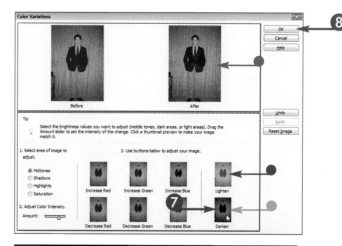

● The result of the adjustment shows up in the After preview.

To increase the effect, click the thumbnail again.

● You can increase the brightness by clicking **Lighten**.

● You can decrease the brightness of the image by clicking **Darken**.

⑦ Continue adjusting other tonal ranges as needed.

⑧ Click **OK**.

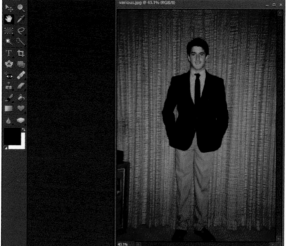

Photoshop Elements makes the color adjustments to the image.

In this example, the subject in the photo is faded and washed out. The Color Variations dialog box enables you to bring out the red tones and increase the shadowing.

How can I undo color adjustments while using the Color Variations dialog box?

● If you have clicked a Decrease thumbnail image, you can click the corresponding **Increase** thumbnail image to undo the effect.

● If you have clicked an Increase thumbnail image, you can click the corresponding **Decrease** thumbnail image to undo the effect.

● Click **Undo** to cancel the last color adjustment.

● Click **Reset Image** to return the image to its original state — as it looked before you opened the dialog box.

Replace a Color

The Replace Color command lets you change one or more colors throughout your image using hue, saturation, and lightness controls.

The Replace Color command is useful for replacing all instances of a color in a photo. To replace small areas of color by brushing, see the section "Replace a Color with a Brush" in Chapter 11.

Replace a Color

① In the Editor, click **Enhance**.

Note: *For details about opening the Editor, see Chapter 1.*

② Click **Adjust Color**.

③ Click **Replace Color**.

To apply color corrections to a particular layer, select the layer before opening the dialog box.

Note: *See Chapter 7 to read more about layers.*

The Replace Color dialog box appears. The mouse pointer (⬚) changes to an eyedropper (🖋).

④ Click in the image to select a color to replace.

● Photoshop Elements turns the selected color to white in the preview window.

⑤ Click and drag the Fuzziness slider (▣) to control the degree of tolerance for related colors within the image or selection.

Dragging to the right selects more color, and dragging to the left selects less color.

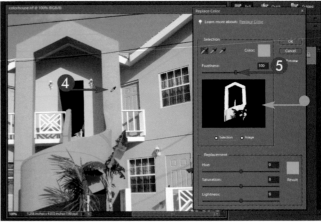

6 Click and drag the sliders to change the colors inside the selected area.

Note: *For details about these controls, see the section "Enhance Colors with Guided Edit."*

7 Click **OK**.

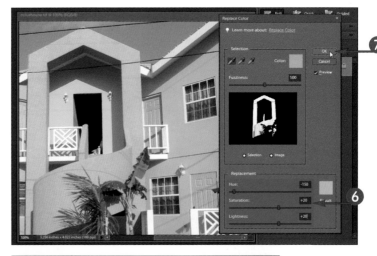

Photoshop Elements replaces the selected color.

TIPS

How can I replace more than one area of color?

In step **4**, you can press Shift and then click inside your image to add other colors to your selection. If you are viewing the Selection preview, the white area inside the preview box increases as you click. To deselect colors from your selection, press Alt and then click a color inside your image.

Can I replace a color in my image using the painting tools?

Yes. For example, you can click the **Paint Bucket** tool (⟨icon⟩), select a Foreground color, and then click to replace a color in your image with the selected color. For more on using Photoshop Elements' painting tools, see Chapter 11.

Equalize Colors

You can use the Equalize filter to redistribute the brightness values in your image. This can lighten an overly dark or gray photo.

Photoshop Elements equalizes an image by finding the lightest and darkest colors in the image and converting them to white and black. It also redistributes the colors in between.

If you make a selection before performing the command, Elements asks whether you want to equalize only the selection or equalize the entire image based on the selection.

Equalize Colors

① In the Editor, click **Filter**.

Note: For details about opening the Editor, see Chapter 1.

② Click **Adjustments**.

③ Click **Equalize**.

Photoshop Elements equalizes the colors in the image.

You can reduce the number of colors in your image using the Posterize filter, which can give a photographic image a solid-color poster look.

If you make a selection before executing the Posterize command, you affect only the selected pixels. Similarly, if you have a multilayered image, your adjustments affect only the selected layer. See Chapter 5 for more on making a selection and Chapter 7 for more on layers.

Posterize Colors

① In the Editor, click **Filter**.

Note: For details about opening the Editor, see Chapter 1.

② Click **Adjustments**.

③ Click **Posterize**.

The Posterize dialog box appears.

④ Type the number of levels.

More levels mean more solid colors in the resulting image.

⑤ Click **OK**.

Photoshop Elements posterizes the image.

Boost Colors with the Multiply Blending Mode

You can use the Multiply blending mode to strengthen and intensify colors in your photo. For example, if environmental light and chemicals have faded a color Polaroid over time, you can scan the image and give it a color boost with the Multiply blending mode. You can control the intensity of the blending mode by setting an opacity level.

Boost Colors with the Multiply Blending Mode

1 In the Editor, duplicate the layer you want to adjust.

Note: *For details about opening the Editor, see Chapter 1.*

● The fastest way to duplicate the layer is to drag and drop the layer over the **Create a New Layer** button (▣).

Note: *See Chapter 7 to read more about layers.*

2 Click here and then click **Multiply**.

Photoshop Elements applies the Multiply blending mode.

③ Click here and then click and drag the slider (▣) to the left to lessen the effect.

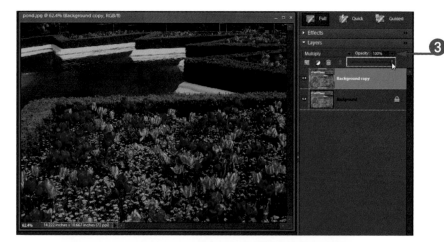

● If a specific area of the layer is too dark, you can click and drag the **Eraser** tool (▨) to undo the Multiply effect.

Note: *For more about the Eraser tool, see Chapter 11.*

TIP

How can I boost an area of pixels rather than an entire layer?

① Select the pixels using a selection tool.

Note: *See Chapter 5 for more on selecting areas of your image.*

② Click **Layer**.

③ Click **New**.

④ Click **Layer via Copy**.

● Photoshop Elements copies the selected pixels to a new layer, to which you can apply the Multiply blending mode.

Turn a Color Photo into Black and White

You can change the image mode to turn a color photo into a black-and-white photo. Elements does this by converting the colors to grayscale. You may want to make a picture black and white to create a dramatic effect or before publishing the photo in a non-color newsletter or brochure.

You may want to copy the color image file before making the change and saving so the full-color original file remains intact. See Chapter 2 to read how to save files.

Turn a Color Photo into Black and White

1 In the Editor, click **Enhance**.

Note: For details about opening the Editor, see Chapter 1.

2 Click **Convert to Black and White**.

The Convert to Black and White dialog box opens.

3 Click a style.

● Photoshop Elements displays a preview of the black-and-white version.

④ You can click the color sliders () to adjust the contributions of the original colors to the final black-and-white version.

⑤ You can click the Contrast slider to increase or decrease the contrast.

⑥ Click **OK**.

Photoshop Elements converts the image to black and white.

TIP

Can I remove color from just one color channel?
Yes. Working with channels allows you to choose which colors will become black and white. You can leave your image in RGB color mode and desaturate the color channels using the Hue/Saturation dialog box.

① Click **Enhance**.

② Click **Adjust Color**.

③ Click **Adjust Hue/Saturation**.

④ In the Hue/Saturation dialog box, click here and then click a color channel.

⑤ Drag the Saturation slider () to the left.

⑥ Click **OK** to desaturate the color channel.

Add Color to a Black-and-White Photo

You can enhance a black-and-white photo by adding color with Elements' painting tools. For example, you can add color to a baby's cheeks or to articles of clothing. To add color, you must first make sure your image's mode is RGB Color.

You can retain the original black-and-white version of your photo by making color changes on duplicate or adjustment layers. See Chapter 7 for more about layers.

Add Color to a Black-and-White Photo

① In the Editor, click **Image**.

Note: For details about opening the Editor, see Chapter 1.

② Click **Mode**.

③ Click **RGB Color**.

If your image has multiple layers, you may need to flatten the layers before proceeding. In the prompt box that appears, click **Flatten** to continue.

④ Duplicate the Background layer.

Note: See Chapter 7 to read more about layers.

⑤ Click the **Brush** tool ().

⑥ Click the Foreground color.

⑦ In the Color Picker dialog box, click a color range.

⑧ Click a color.

⑨ Click **OK**.

10 Set the blending mode to **Color**. This enables you to retain the lighting details of the objects that you paint over.

11 Click and drag to paint the color on the photo.

Photoshop Elements applies the color to the black-and-white image.

To confine the effect to a particular area, you can make a selection prior to applying the tool. See Chapter 5 for more about making selections.

This example shows color added to a pair of pants.

How do I tone down a layer color?

You can change the layer opacity in the Layers palette to make the color more transparent. Follow these steps:

1 Click the layer containing the color you want to edit.

2 Click here and then click and drag the slider (▣) that appears.

● Photoshop Elements automatically adjusts the color as you drag.

Note: See Chapter 7 to read more about layers.

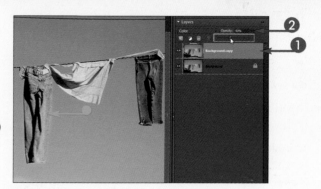

Adjust Color Using Color Curves

You can manipulate the tones and contrast of your image with the Color Curves dialog box. In the dialog box, the colors in the image are represented by a sloping line graph. The top-right part of the line represents the highlights, the middle part the midtones, and the bottom-left the shadows.

You can adjust curves in just a part of your image by making a selection or selecting a layer before executing the command. For more on making selections, see Chapter 5. For more on working with layers, see Chapter 7.

Adjust Colors Using Color Curves

① In the Editor, click **Enhance**.

Note: For details about opening the Editor, see Chapter 1.

② Click **Adjust Color**.

③ Click **Adjust Color Curves**.

● In this example, a selection was made with the Elliptical marquee (⬚).

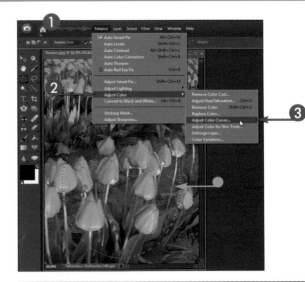

The Adjust Color Curves dialog box appears.

④ Click a style.

● Photoshop Elements displays a preview of the adjusted version.

● The curves graph changes depending on the style.

In this example, choosing the Increase Contrast style gives the graph a slight S shape.

⑤ You can click sliders (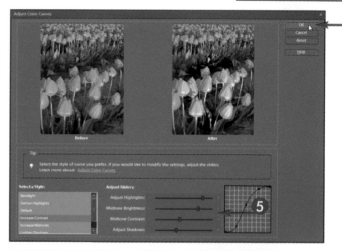) to make more adjustments to the tones and contrast in the image.

⑥ Click **OK**.

Photoshop Elements applies the adjustment to the image.

N

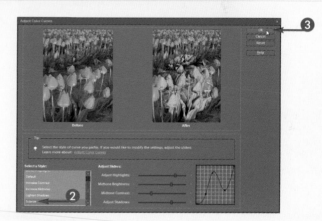

TIP

How can I give the colors in my image an out-of-this-world appearance?

You can choose the Solarize style in the Color Curves dialog box:

① Follow steps **1** to **3** in this task.

② Click **Solarize** in the Select a Style menu.

③ Click **OK** to apply the effect.

Note: *Photoshop Elements also has a Solarize filter that creates a similar effect. See Chapter 12 for more about filters.*

Painting and Drawing on Photos

Want to add extra elements to your photos, such as lines, shapes, or solid areas of color? Photoshop Elements offers a variety of tools you can use to paint and draw on your images as well as add shapes and colors. This chapter introduces you to a few of those tools and their many uses.

Set the Foreground and Background Colors

You can select colors to use with many of the painting and drawing tools in Photoshop Elements by setting the foreground and background colors. The Brush and Pencil tools apply the foreground color, and the Eraser tool applies the background color.

See the section "Add Color with the Brush Tool" for more on how to paint on a photo. See the section "Erase an Area" for more on using the Eraser.

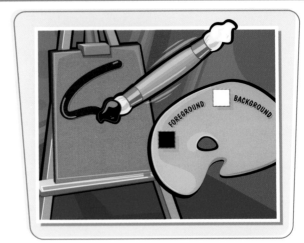

Set the Foreground and Background Colors

SET THE FOREGROUND COLOR

① In the Editor, click the **Foreground Color** box (■).

Note: For details about opening the Editor, see Chapter 1.

The Color Picker dialog box appears.

② Click and drag the color slider (▶) to select a color range.

③ Click a color.

④ Click **OK**.

● The selected color appears in the Foreground Color box.

● When you use a tool that applies the foreground color, Photoshop Elements paints or draws the foreground color on the photo.

This example uses the Brush tool.

SET THE BACKGROUND COLOR

1 Click the **Background Color** box ().

The Color Picker dialog box appears.

2 Click and drag the color slider (▶) to select a color range.

3 Click a color.

4 Click **OK**.

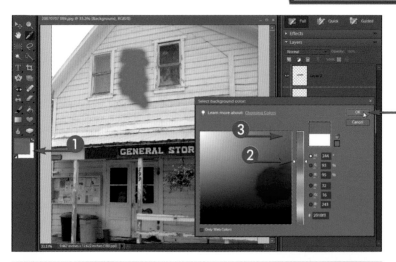

● When you use a tool that applies the background color, such as the Eraser tool, Photoshop Elements applies the Background color on the photo.

The Eraser tool applies color only in the Background layer; in other layers, the eraser turns pixels transparent.

Note: See Chapter 7 for more about layers.

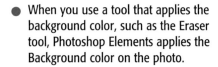

How do I reset the foreground and background colors?

Click the **Default** button (◻) to the lower left of the Foreground and Background color boxes. Doing so resets the colors to black and white. You can also click the **Switch** button (↻) or press X to swap the foreground and background colors.

Does Photoshop Elements offer a set of common colors?

Yes. You can select a color to paint or draw on your photo from the Swatches palette, which includes a set of commonly used colors. To view the palette, click **Window** and then **Color Swatches**. You can click the color you want to use, and the Foreground Color box in the toolbox immediately reflects your choice.

Add Color with the Brush Tool

You can use the Brush tool to add patches of solid color to your image. You can use the tool to cover unwanted elements or change the appearance of clothing or a backdrop. When applying the Brush tool, you can control the size of the brush strokes by choosing a brush size. For realistic results, turn on the Airbrush feature to apply a softer line of color.

To limit where the brush applies color, create a selection before using the tool. For details, see Chapter 5.

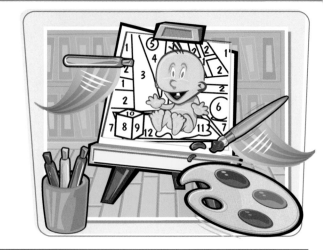

Add Color with the Brush Tool

1 In the Editor, click the **Brush** tool (🖌).

Note: *For details about opening the Editor, see Chapter 1.*

2 Click the **Foreground Color** box (■) to select a color with which to paint.

Note: *For details, see the section "Set the Foreground and Background Colors."*

3 Click here and then click a brush size and type.

● To set a brush size, you can also click here and adjust the slider that appears.

4 Press Enter to close the Brushes menu.

5 Click and drag the mouse pointer (○) on the image.

Photoshop Elements applies color to the image.

6 Click here to reduce the opacity of the paint effect.

7 Click and drag the mouse pointer (○) on the image.

Photoshop Elements applies transparent color to the image.

To undo the most recent brush stroke, you can click **Edit** and then **Undo Brush Tool** or click the **Undo** button (↶).

TIPS

How do I paint thin lines?

Use the Pencil tool (✏), which is similar to the Brush tool (🖌) except that it paints only thin, hard-edged lines. Like the Paintbrush, the Pencil applies the foreground color. See the section "Draw a Line" for more on using the Pencil tool.

What can I do with the Impressionist Brush tool?

The Impressionist Brush (🖌) creates artistic effects by blending existing colors in an image together. The Impressionist Brush does not add any foreground or background color to your image. You can select the tool from the menu that appears when you click and hold the **Brush** tool (🖌).

Change Brush Styles

You can select from a variety of predefined brush styles in Photoshop Elements to apply color to your image in different ways. You can also create a custom brush style by specifying spacing, fade, and other characteristics for your brush.

Change Brush Styles

SELECT FROM A PREDEFINED SET

1. In the Editor, click the **Brush** tool (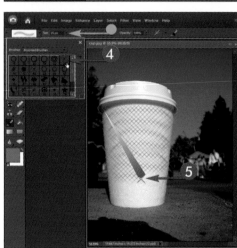).

Note: For details about opening the Editor, see Chapter 1.

2. Click here to display the brushes window.

3. Click here and then click a set of brushes.

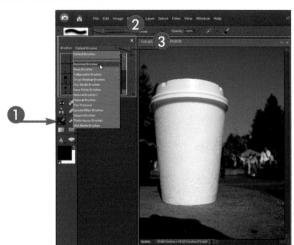

The set appears in the Brushes menu.

4. Click a brush style to select it.

The mouse pointer changes to the new brush shape.

● You can click here to adjust the brush size.

5. Click and drag the brush on the photo.

Photoshop Elements applies the brush to the area.

Note: To apply the brush, see the section "Add Color with the Brush Tool."

CUSTOMIZE A BRUSH

① Click the **More Options** button ().

A palette of brush options appears.

② Click and drag the sliders (🔲) or type values to define the new brush attributes.

● You can limit the length of your brush strokes with the Fade slider.

● You can randomize the painted color with the Hue Jitter slider.

● You can change the shape of the brush tip by clicking and dragging here.

● The brush style appears in the Brushes menu.

③ Click and drag the brush on the photo.

Photoshop Elements applies the customized brush to the area.

Note: *For more about applying the brush, see the section "Add Color with the Brush Tool."*

TIP

How can I make a brush apply dots instead of a line?

① Click the **More Options** button (🖌) to open the More Options settings in the Options bar.

② Click and drag the slider (🔲) to increase the Spacing value to greater than 100%.

● When you click and drag a round brush shape, you get dots instead of a contiguous line.

Add Color with the Paint Bucket Tool

The Paint Bucket tool lets you fill areas in your image with solid color. You can use this technique to change the color of clothes, the sky, backgrounds, and more. By default, when you apply the Paint Bucket tool, it affects adjacent pixels in the image. You can set the Paint Bucket's Tolerance value to determine the range of colors the paint bucket affects when you apply it.

Add Color with the Paint Bucket Tool

① In the Editor, click the **Paint Bucket** tool ().

Note: For details about opening the Editor, see Chapter 1.

② Click the **Foreground Color** box (■) to select a color for painting.

Note: For details, see the section "Set the Foreground and Background Colors."

③ Type a Tolerance value from 0 to 255.

To paint over a narrow range of colors, type a small value; to paint over a wide range of colors, type a large value.

④ Click inside the image.

Photoshop Elements fills an area of the image with the foreground color.

CHANGE IMAGE OPACITY

1 To fill an area with semitransparent color, type a percentage value of less than 100% in the Opacity field.

2 Click inside the image.

Photoshop Elements fills an area with see-through paint.

FILL NONCONTIGUOUS AREAS

1 To fill noncontiguous but similar areas throughout the image, click to deselect **Contiguous** (☑ changes to ■).

2 Click inside the selection.

Photoshop Elements fills similar areas of the image, even if they are not contiguous with the clicked pixel.

How can I reset a tool to the default settings?
You can reset a tool using a command in the Options bar:

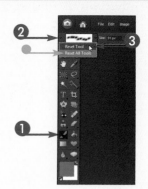

1 Click the tool in the toolbox.

2 Click **Reset** (■) on the far-left side of the Options bar.

3 Click **Reset Tool** from the menu that appears.

For painting tools, this resets the opacity to 100%, the blending mode to Normal, and other attributes to their startup values.

● You can click **Reset All Tools** from the menu to reset all the Elements tools to their default settings.

Replace a Color with a Brush

You can replace colors in your image with the current foreground color using the Color Replacement tool. This gives you a free-form way of recoloring objects in your image while keeping the shading on the objects intact.

The Color Replacement tool is useful for replacing specific areas of color. To quickly replace a color that occurs throughout a photo, see the section "Replace a Color" in Chapter 10.

Replace a Color with a Brush

① In the Editor, click and hold the **Brush** tool ().

Note: For details about opening the Editor, see Chapter 1.

② From the list that appears, click **Color Replacement Tool** (■).

③ Click the **Foreground Color** box (■) to select a color for painting.

④ Click here and select a brush size and type.

⑤ Click the **Sampling: Continuous** button (■).

Sampling: Continuous samples different colors to replace as you paint.

● Sampling: Once (■) samples only the first color you click.

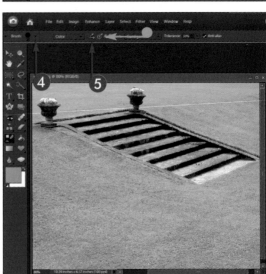

6 Type a tolerance from 1% to 100%.

The greater the tolerance, the greater the range of colors the tool replaces.

7 Click and drag in your image.

Photoshop Elements replaces color.

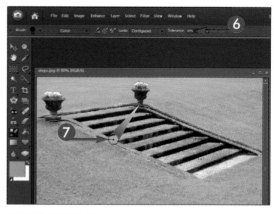

8 Continue to click and drag in your image.

Photoshop Elements replaces more color.

TIP

How do I fill a selection with a color?

You can use the Fill command to fill a selection with a solid or semitransparent color. Filling is an easy way to change the color of an object in your image.

1 Click **Edit**.

2 Click **Fill Selection**.

The Fill Layer dialog box opens.

3 Select the color you want to fill with and set an opacity for the fill color.

4 Click **OK**.

● Photoshop Elements fills the selection.

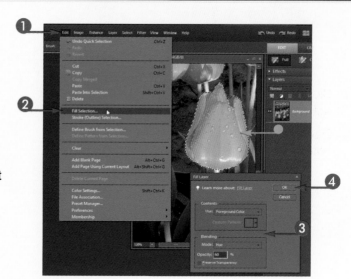

Draw a Shape

You can create solid shapes in your image using Photoshop Elements' many shape tools. Shapes offer an easy way to add whimsical objects, labels, or buttons to an image.

When you add a shape to an image, Elements places the shape in its own layer. This makes it easy to move and transform the shape later on. Because shape objects are vector graphics in Elements, they can be resized without a loss in quality. For more information about layers, see Chapter 7.

Draw a Shape

① In the Editor, click and hold the **Rectangle** tool (▢).

Note: For details about opening the Editor, see Chapter 1.

② Click **Custom Shape Tool** (♥) in the menu that appears.

The Custom Shape tool shares space in the toolbox with the other shape tools.

Note: See Chapter 1 for more about working with toolbox tools.

③ Click here to open the Custom Shapes menu.

④ Click a shape.

⑤ Press Enter to close the menu.

⑥ Click here and then click a color for your shape.

⑦ Press **Enter** to close the menu.

● You can click here to select a 3-D style for your shape.

⑧ Click and drag your mouse pointer (✛) to draw the shape.

● Photoshop Elements places the shape in its own layer.

Note: *For more about layers, see Chapter 7.*

 TIP

How do I resize a shape after I draw it?

① Click the shape's layer.

② Click the **Custom Shape** tool ().

③ Click **Image**.

④ Click **Transform Shape**.

⑤ Click a transform command.

You can then resize the shape just like you would a selection.

Note: *See the section "Skew or Distort a Selection" in Chapter 6 for more details on transformations.*

Draw a Line

You can draw all kinds of lines on your image using several different tools. Photoshop Elements' Line tool lets you draw a straight line. You can customize the line with arrows, giving you an easy way to point out elements in your image. You can also draw free-form lines with the Pencil tool.

When you add a line to an image with the Line tool, Elements places the line in its own layer. This makes it easy to move and transform the line later on. Because line objects are vector graphics in Elements, they can be resized without a loss in quality. For more information about layers, see Chapter 7.

Draw a Line

DRAW A LINE WITH THE LINE TOOL

1. In the Editor, click and hold the **Rectangle** tool (□).

Note: For details about opening the Editor, see Chapter 1.

2. Click **Line Tool** (◥).

3. Click here and then click **Start** or **End** to include arrowheads on your line (■ changes to ✓).

● You can also specify the shape of the arrowheads by typing values here.

4. Press **Enter** to close the Arrowheads window.

5. Type a line weight.

6. Click here to select a different line color.

● You can click here to set a style for your line.

7. Press **Enter** to close the menu.

8. Click and drag your mouse pointer (+) to draw the line.

● Photoshop Elements places the line in its own layer.

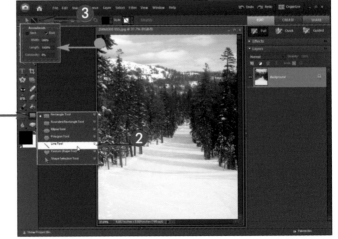

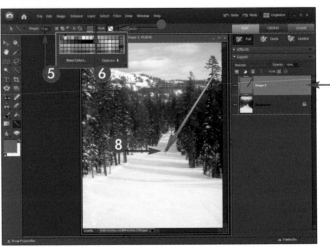

DRAW A LINE WITH THE PENCIL TOOL

① Click the layer in which you want to draw the pencil line.

② Click and hold the **Brush** tool (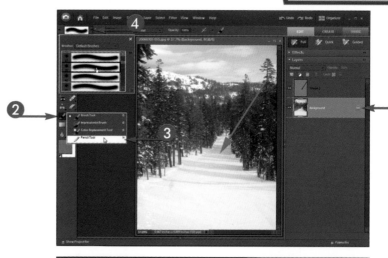).

③ Click **Pencil Tool** ( ) in the menu that appears.

④ Click here and then click a line brush shape or style.

● You can also set a line width here.

⑤ Click and drag to draw a free-form line.

A line appears on the image.

TIP

Can I add an outline along a selection in my image?

① Click **Edit** and then click **Stroke (Outline) Selection**.

The Stroke dialog box opens.

② Type a width for the line.

● You can click here to select a color for the line.

③ Click a location and then click **OK**.

● Photoshop Elements applies the stroke.

Erase an Area

You can use the Eraser tool to erase unwanted areas of your photo. When you apply the Eraser tool in the background layer, the erased pixels are replaced with the current Background color. When you erase in other layers, the eraser turns the pixels transparent, revealing any underlying layers.

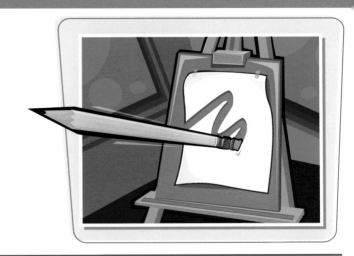

Erase an Area

1 In the Editor, click the **Eraser** tool (![icon]).

Note: For details about opening the Editor, see Chapter 1.

2 Click the **Background Color** box (![icon]) to select a color to appear in place of the erased pixels.

Note: For details, see the section "Set the Foreground and Background Colors."

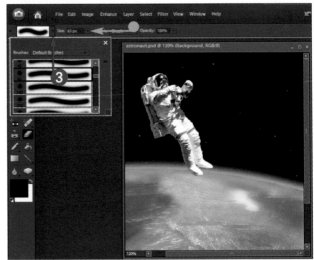

3 Click here and then click an eraser size and type.

● You can also click here and adjust the slider to set an eraser size.

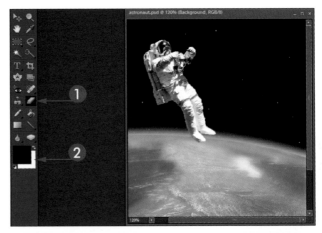

ERASE THE BACKGROUND LAYER

④ Click the Background layer.

⑤ Click and drag the mouse pointer (◯) to erase.

Portions of the Background layer are erased and replaced with the background color.

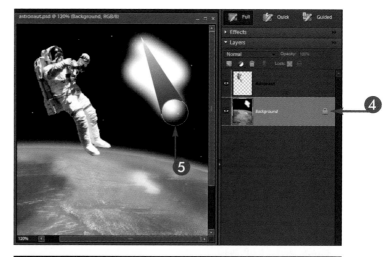

ERASE A NORMAL LAYER

⑥ Click a normal layer.

⑦ Click and drag the mouse pointer (◯) to erase.

Portions of the layer are erased to reveal the underlying layer.

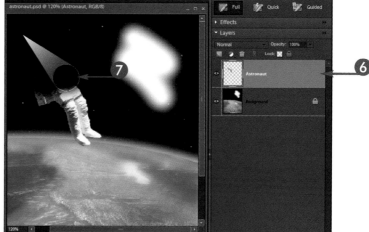

TIPS

What do the other eraser types do?

You can click and hold the **Eraser** tool (◩) to access other eraser types. You can use the Background Eraser tool (◩) to sample a color in your image and erase only that color as you drag the tool over your image. The Magic Eraser tool (◩) erases all the adjacent, similarly colored pixels when you click it.

Which eraser mode should I use?

In the Options bar, you can choose from three eraser modes: Brush, Pencil, and Block. Brush mode, which is the default mode, enables you to apply the eraser to your image like a paintbrush. The Pencil mode acts like a pencil eraser. The Block mode turns the eraser mouse pointer into a square shape for erasing.

You can apply a *gradient*, which is a blend from one color to another, to give objects in your image a radiant or 3-D look. You can apply a gradient to a selected portion of an image or the entire image.

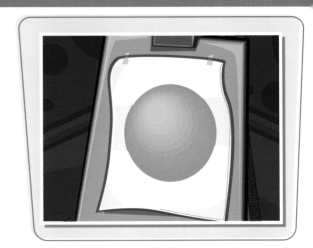

Apply a Gradient

1 In the Editor, make a selection.

Note: *For details about opening the Editor, see Chapter 1. See Chapter 5 for more on making selections.*

2 Click the **Gradient** tool (▢).

● A linear gradient is the default. You can select different geometries in the Options bar.

3 Click the gradient swatch.

The Gradient Editor opens.

4 Click a preset gradient type from the top box.

● You can define a custom gradient by changing these settings.

5 Click **OK**.

⑥ Click and drag the mouse pointer (+) inside the selection.

This defines the direction and transition of the gradient.

Dragging a long line with the tool produces a gradual transition.

Dragging a short line with the tool produces an abrupt transition.

Photoshop Elements generates a gradient inside the selection.

TIP

How can I highlight an object in my image using a gradient?

① Place the object in its own layer.

② Create a new layer below the object. Select the new layer.

③ Click the **Gradient** tool (▢).

④ Click the **Radial Gradient** button (▢).

⑤ Click and drag the mouse pointer (+) from the center of the object outward to create the gradient.

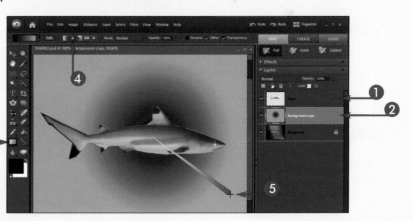

CHAPTER 12

Applying Filters

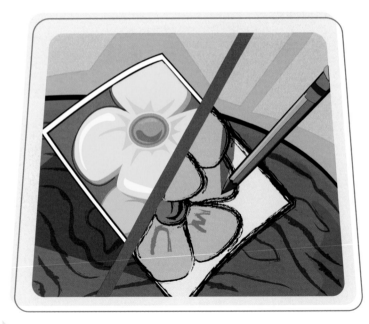

With Photoshop Elements' filters, you can quickly and easily apply enhancements to your image, including artistic effects, texture effects, and distortions. Filters can help you correct defects in your images or let you turn a photograph into something resembling an impressionist painting. This chapter highlights a few of Photoshop Elements' 100+ filters. For details about all the filters, see the Help documentation.

You can use the Blur filters to apply a variety of blurring effects to your photos. For example, you can use the Gaussian Blur filter to obscure background objects while keeping foreground objects in focus.

Blurring a busy background makes an image look as if it has a short depth of field. A short depth of field keeps the foreground subject in focus while placing the background out of focus.

Blur an Image

1. In the Editor, select the layer to which you want to apply the filter.

Note: For details about opening the Editor, see Chapter 1. For more about layers, see Chapter 7.

Note: To apply the filter to just part of your image, select an element using a selection tool. For more on selection tools, see Chapter 5.

2. Click **Filter**.

3. Click **Blur**.

4. Click **Gaussian Blur**.

The Gaussian Blur dialog box appears.

● A small preview area shows the filter's effect.

5. Click minus or plus (— or +) to zoom out or in.

6. Click to select the **Preview** option to preview the effect in the main window (■ changes to ✓).

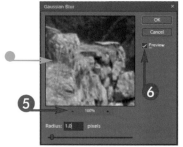

7 Click and drag the Radius slider (▣) to control the amount of blur added.

In this example, boosting the Radius value increases the amount of blur.

8 Click **OK**.

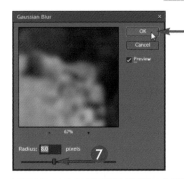

Elements applies the filter.

In this example, the Background layer is blurred while the foreground remains unchanged.

Note: *For details about sharpening an image, see Chapter 8.*

TIP

How do I add directional blurring to an image?

1 Select the layer to blur.

2 Click **Filter**.

3 Click **Blur**.

4 Click **Motion Blur**.

5 In the Motion Blur dialog box, click and drag the Angle dial to define the direction of the blur.

6 Click and drag the slider (▣) to adjust the amount of blur.

7 Click **OK** to apply the filter.

Distort an Image

You can use any of the Distort filters to stretch and squeeze your image, creating the appearance of waves, glass, swirls, and more. For example, the Twirl filter turns the image into a swirl of colors, and the Zig Zag filter adds wavelike ripples.

To apply the filter to just part of your image, select an element using a selection tool. For more on selection tools, see Chapter 5.

Distort an Image

① In the Editor, select the layer to which you want to apply the filter.

Note: *For details about opening the Editor, see Chapter 1. For more about layers, see Chapter 7.*

② Click **Filter**.

③ Click **Distort**.

④ Click an effect.

The filter's dialog box appears.

⑤ Make adjustments to the filter's settings to fine-tune the effect.

With some filters, you can preview the effect before applying it to the image.

⑥ Click **OK**.

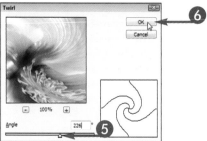

Elements applies the filter.

In this example, the Twirl distortion filter is applied.

In this example, the Zig Zag distortion filter is applied.

TIPS

How many filters does Photoshop Elements offer?

Photoshop Elements has 105 filters grouped into 14 categories. You can experiment with each one to find out what effect it has on your image. One of the more popular filters is Lighting Effects, which creates the illusion of spotlights and other specialized illumination in your photos. See Chapter 9 for details on Lighting Effects. You can also add filters to stylize your text. See Chapter 13 for more on that subject.

Is there another way to distort a selection?

Yes. You can use the Distort command to reshape a selected element in your photo. After selecting the element, click **Image**, **Transform**, and then **Distort**. Photoshop Elements surrounds the selection with handles, which you can drag to distort the element. See Chapter 6 for more about distorting selections.

Turn an Image into a Painting

You can use many of Photoshop Elements' Artistic filters to make your image look as if you created it with a paintbrush or other art media. The Watercolor filter, for example, applies a painted effect by converting similarly colored areas in your image to solid colors.

To apply the filter to just part of your image, select an element using a selection tool. For more on selection tools, see Chapter 5.

Turn an Image into a Painting

1 In the Editor, select the layer to which you want to apply the filter.

Note: For details about opening the Editor, see Chapter 1. For more about layers, see Chapter 7.

In this example, the image has a single Background layer.

2 Click **Filter**.

3 Click **Artistic**.

4 Click an effect.

The Filter Gallery dialog box appears.

5 Adjust the filter's settings to fine-tune the effect.

● With some filters, you can preview the effect before applying it to the image. Click minus or plus ([−] or [+]) to zoom out or in.

6 Click **OK**.

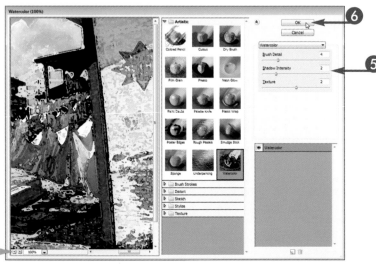

Elements applies the filter. In this example, the Watercolor filter is applied.

In this example, the Cutout filter is applied.

TIP

How do I make my image look like a sponge painting?
You can use the Sponge filter to reduce details and modify the image's shapes:

1 Follow steps **1** to **4** in this section, but select **Sponge** in step **4**.

2 In the Sponge dialog box, click and drag the sliders (⬛) to define the size and contrast of the sponge strokes.

3 Click **OK**, and Photoshop Elements applies the filter.

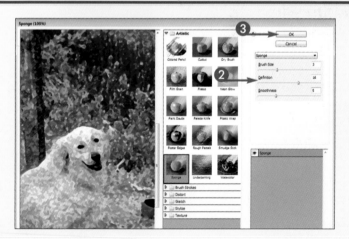

Turn an Image into a Sketch

The Sketch filters add outlining effects to your image. The Charcoal filter, for example, makes an image look as if you sketched it using charcoal on paper.

The Charcoal filter uses the foreground color as the charcoal color and the background color as the paper color. Changing these colors alters the filter's effect. For more on adjusting colors, see Chapter 10.

To apply the filter to just part of your image, select an element using a selection tool. For more on selection tools, see Chapter 5.

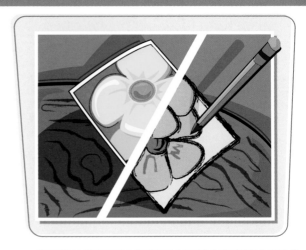

Turn an Image into a Sketch

① In the Editor, select the foreground and background colors that you want to apply in your sketch.

Note: *For details about opening the Editor, see Chapter 1. For details on how to select colors, see Chapter 11.*

② Select the layer to which you want to apply the filter.

Note: *For more about layers, see Chapter 7.*

In this example, the image has a single Background layer.

③ Click **Filter**.

④ Click **Sketch**.

⑤ Click **Charcoal**.

The Charcoal dialog box appears.

A window displays a preview of the filter's effect.

⑥ Click minus or plus (- or +) to zoom out or in.

⑦ Click and drag the sliders (▣) to control the filter's effect.

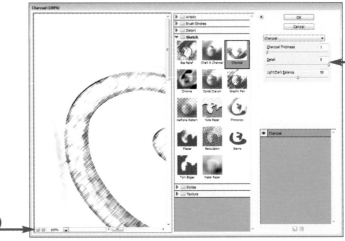

In this example, the thickness of the charcoal strokes has increased and the detail has decreased.

⑧ Click **OK**.

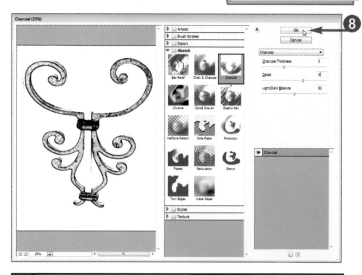

Photoshop Elements applies the filter.

TIP

What does the Photocopy filter do?

The Photocopy filter converts your image's shadows and midtones to the foreground color and converts highlights to the background color to make the image look like a photocopy.

① Follow steps **1** to **4** in this section, selecting **Photocopy** in step **4**.

② In the Photocopy dialog box, click and drag the sliders (▣) to control the detail and darkness of the colors.

③ Click **OK**, and Photoshop Elements applies the filter.

Add Noise
to an Image

Filters in the Noise menu add graininess to or remove it from your image. You can add graininess with the Add Noise filter.

To apply the filter to just part of your image, select an element using a selection tool. For more on selection tools, see Chapter 5.

Add Noise to an Image

① In the Editor, select the layer to which you want to apply the filter.

Note: *For details about opening the Editor, see Chapter 1. For more about layers, see Chapter 7.*

In this example, the image has a single Background layer.

② Click **Filter**.

③ Click **Noise**.

④ Click **Add Noise**.

The Add Noise dialog box appears, displaying a preview of the effect.

⑤ Click minus or plus (─ or ＋) to zoom out or in.

⑥ Click to select the **Preview** option to preview the effect in the main window (■ changes to ✓).

7 Click and drag the Amount slider (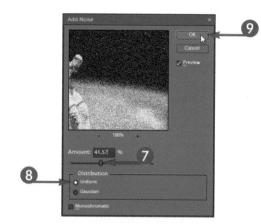) to change the noise.

In this example, the Amount value has been increased.

8 Click here to select how you want the noise distributed (● changes to ○).

The Uniform option spreads the noise more evenly than Gaussian.

9 Click **OK**.

Photoshop Elements applies the filter.

(TIPS)

What does the Monochromatic setting in the Add Noise dialog box do?

If you click to select **Monochromatic** (■ changes to ☑), Elements adds noise by lightening or darkening pixels in your image. Pixel hues stay the same. At high settings with the Monochromatic setting on, the filter produces a television-static effect.

Can you apply filters from an Elements palette?

Yes. If you open the Effects palette and click **Filters** (■), you can access most of the filters that are also found under the Filter menu. You can choose different filter categories from the palette menu.

EFFECTS

- Blur
- Dry Brush
- Pinch
- Add Noise
- Charcoal Sketch

The Pixelate filters divide areas of your image into solid-colored dots or shapes. The Crystallize filter, one example of a Pixelate filter, re-creates your image using colored polygons.

To apply the filter to just part of your image, select an element using a selection tool. For more on selection tools, see Chapter 5.

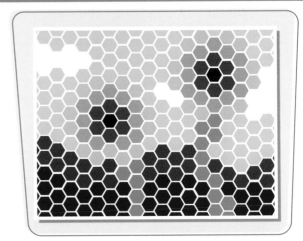

Pixelate an Image

① In the Editor, select the layer to which you want to apply the filter.

Note: *For details about opening the Editor, see Chapter 1. For more about layers, see Chapter 7.*

In this example, the image has a single Background layer.

② Click **Filter**.

③ Click **Pixelate**.

④ Click **Crystallize**.

The Crystallize dialog box appears, displaying a preview of the filter's effect.

⑤ Click minus or plus (☐ or ☐) to zoom out or in.

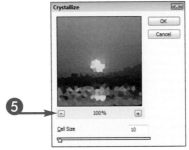

⑥ Click and drag the Cell Size slider (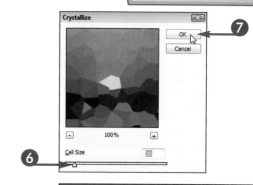)
to adjust the size of the shapes.

The size can range from 3 to 300.

In this example, the Cell Size has
been increased slightly.

⑦ Click **OK**.

Photoshop Elements applies the filter.

TIP

What does the Mosaic filter do?
The Mosaic filter converts your image
to a set of solid-color squares.

① Click **Filter**.

② Click **Pixelate**.

③ Click **Mosaic**.

The Mosaic dialog box opens.

④ Click and drag the slider (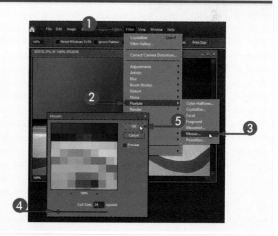) to
specify the mosaic square size.

⑤ Click **OK** to apply the filter.

Emboss an Image

You can achieve the effect of a three-dimensional shape pressed into paper with the Emboss filter. You may find this filter useful for generating textured backgrounds.

To apply the filter to just part of your image, select an element using a selection tool. For more on selection tools, see Chapter 5.

Emboss an Image

1 In the Editor, select the layer to which you want to apply the filter.

Note: *For details about opening the Editor, see Chapter 1. For more about layers, see Chapter 7.*

In this example, the image has a single Background layer.

2 Click **Filter**.

3 Click **Stylize**.

4 Click **Emboss**.

The Emboss dialog box appears.

Photoshop Elements displays a small preview of the effect.

5 Click minus or plus (□ or ±) to zoom out or in.

6 Type an angle value to specify the direction of the shadow.

● You can also click and drag the Angle dial to set an angle.

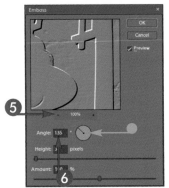

⑦ Click and drag the Height slider (■) to the desired pixel height.

You can specify a height from 1 to 100 to set the strength of the embossing.

⑧ Click and drag the Amount slider (■) to set the amount of embossing detail.

You can specify an amount from 1 to 500 to set the number of edges the filter affects.

⑨ Click **OK**.

Photoshop Elements applies the filter.

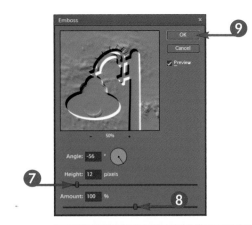

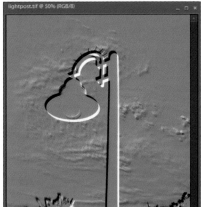

TIP

Do I have another way to create an embossed effect in an image?
Yes. You can use the Bas Relief filter to get a similar effect.

① Follow steps **1** to **4** in this section, clicking **Sketch** in step **3** and **Bas Relief** in step **4**.

② In the Bas Relief dialog box, click and drag the slider (■) to control the detail.

③ Click and drag the slider to control the smoothness.

④ Click **OK**, and Photoshop Elements applies the filter.

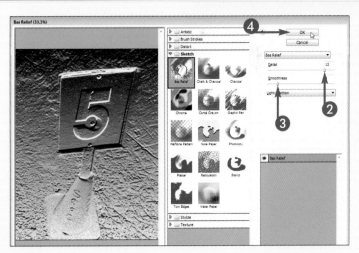

Apply Multiple Filters

You can apply more than one filter to an image using the Filter Gallery interface. The interface enables you to view a variety of filter effects and apply them in combination.

Many filters open the Filter Gallery interface when you apply them, including the Charcoal Sketch filter, which is covered earlier in this chapter.

Note that not all of the effects listed under the Filter menu appear in the Filter Gallery.

Apply Multiple Filters

① In the Editor, select the layer to which you want to apply the filters.

Note: For details about opening the Editor, see Chapter 1.

In this example, the image has a single Background layer.

To apply the filters to just part of your image, make a selection with a selection tool.

② Click **Filter**.

③ Click **Filter Gallery**.

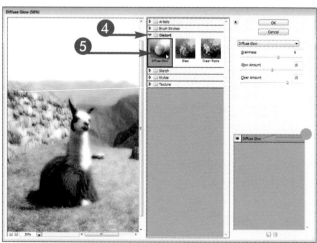

The Filter Gallery dialog box appears with the most recently applied filter selected.

The left pane displays a preview of the filtered image.

④ Click here to display the filters in a category (▶ changes to ▼).

⑤ Click a thumbnail to apply a filter.

● The filter appears in the filter list.

6 Click the **New Effect Layer** button (▧).

● The new effect appears in the list.

7 Click the arrow (▶) to display filters from another category.

8 Click a thumbnail to apply another filter.

You can repeat steps **6** to **8** to apply additional filters.

9 Click **OK**.

Elements applies the filters.

Note: For more about layers, see Chapter 7. For more on using the selection tools, see Chapter 5.

TIP

How can I turn off filters in the Filter Gallery?
Applied filters are listed in the lower-right corner of the Filter Gallery. You can click the **Layer Visibility** icon (👁) to temporarily hide a filter in the list. A hidden filter's effects are not applied to the preview in the left pane of the Filter Gallery, nor are they applied to the image when you click **OK**. You can click the **Trash** icon (🗑) to delete a filter entirely from the list.

Adding Text Elements

Do you want to add letters and words to your photos and illustrations? Photoshop Elements lets you add text to your images and precisely control the appearance and layout of the text. You can also stylize your text using Elements' filters and other tools.

Adding text enables you to label elements in your image or use letters and words in artistic ways. When you add text, it appears in its own layer. You can manipulate text layers in your image to move or stylize the text.

Add Text

1. In the Editor, click the **Horizontal Type** tool (T).

Note: For details about opening the Editor, see Chapter 1.

2. Click where you want the new text to begin.

3. Click here and then select a font, style, and size for your text.

4. Click here to open the color swatches.

5. Click a color for your text.

6 Type your text.

To create a line break, press Enter.

7 When you finish typing your text, click ✓ or press Enter on your keyboard's number pad.

● You can click ⊘ or press Esc to cancel.

● Photoshop Elements places the text in its own layer.

TIPS

How do I reposition my text?

You can move the layer that contains the text with the Move tool (▶). Click the layer of text, click the **Move** tool, and then click and drag to reposition your text. For more on moving a layer, see Chapter 7.

How do I add vertical text to my image?

Click and hold the **Horizontal Type** tool (T), then click **Vertical Type Tool** (T) in the menu that appears. You can also click the Vertical Type tool in the Options bar. Your text will appear with a vertical orientation.

You can change the orientation of existing text in your image by selecting a text layer and clicking the **Change the text orientation** button (T). This converts horizontal text to vertical text and vice versa.

Change the Formatting of Text

You can change the font, style, size, and other characteristics of your text. This can help emphasize or de-emphasize your text.

Change the Formatting of Text

1 In the Editor, click the **Horizontal Type** tool (T).

Note: *For details about opening the Editor or opening palettes, see Chapter 1.*

2 Click the text layer that you want to edit.

3 Click and drag to select some text from the selected layer.

● You can double-click the layer thumbnail to select all the text.

4 Click here and select a font.

5 Click here and select the text's style.

6 Click here and select the text's size.

7 Click the **Anti-Aliased** button (🔤) to control the text's anti-aliasing.

8 When you finish formatting your text, click ☑ or press `Enter` on your keyboard's number pad.

● You can click 🚫 or press `Esc` to cancel.

Photoshop Elements applies the formatting to your text.

TIPS

What is anti-aliasing?

Anti-aliasing is the process of adding semitransparent pixels to curved edges in digital images to make the edges appear smoother. You can apply anti-aliasing to text to improve its appearance. Text that you do not anti-alias can sometimes look jagged. You can control the presence and style of your text's anti-aliasing with the Options bar. Note that at very small text sizes, anti-aliasing can be counterproductive and cause blurring.

How do I change the alignment of my text?

When creating your text, click one of the three alignment buttons: **Left align text** (▤), **Center text** (▤), or **Right align text** (▤). You may find these options useful when you create multiline passages of text.

Change the Color of Text

You can change the color of your text to make it blend or contrast with the rest of the image. You can change the color of all or just part of your text.

Change the Color of Text

1 In the Editor, click the **Horizontal Type** tool (T).

Note: For details about opening the Editor or opening palettes, see Chapter 1.

2 Click the text layer that you want to edit.

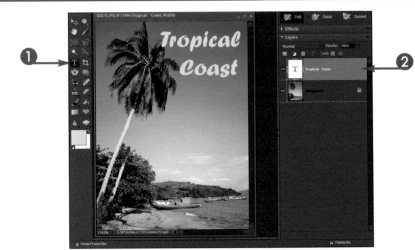

3 Click and drag to select some text.

● You can double-click the layer thumbnail to select all the text.

④ Click here and then click a color.

When you position your mouse pointer (🖑) over a color, it changes to an eyedropper (🖋).

● You can click **More Colors** to open the Color Picker dialog box for more color options.

⑤ Press Enter on your keyboard's number pad.

⑥ Click ✓ or press Enter on your keyboard's number pad again.

● You can click ⊘ or press Esc to cancel.

Photoshop Elements changes the text to the new color.

TIP

How do I change type color using the Color Swatches palette?

① Click the text layer in the Layers palette.

② Click and drag in the image window to select the text you want to recolor.

③ Click a color in the Color Swatches palette.

Note: For details about how to open the Layers and Swatches palettes, see Chapter 1.

The text changes color.

To see the actual new color, deselect it by clicking away from the type in the image window.

Apply a Filter to Text

You can add interesting effects to your text with Elements' filters. To apply a filter to text, you must first simplify it. *Simplifying* converts your type layer into a regular Elements layer. You can no longer edit simplified text using the text tools.

For more about filters, see Chapter 12.

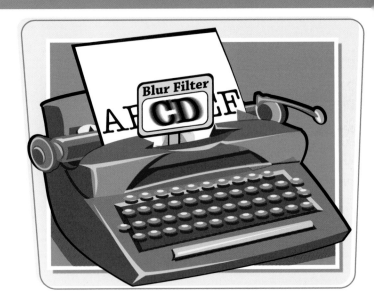

Apply a Filter to Text

1. In the Editor, select the text layer to which you want to apply a filter.

   Note: *For details about opening the Editor or opening palettes, see Chapter 1.*

2. Click **Filter**.

3. Click a filter submenu.

4. Click a filter.

A dialog box appears asking if you want to simplify the layer.

5. Click **OK**.

● Photoshop Elements converts the text layer to a regular layer.

Note: To keep a copy of your editable text layer, you can duplicate it before applying the filter. See Chapter 7 for details.

6 Specify your filter settings.

Note: For more information on filter settings, see Chapter 12.

7 Click **OK**.

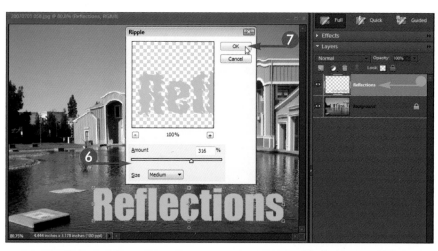

Photoshop Elements applies the filter to the text.

This example adds a distortion effect to the text with the Ripple filter.

TIPS

How can I create semitransparent text?

Select the text layer in the Layers palette and then reduce the layer's opacity to less than 100%. This makes the type semitransparent. For details about changing opacity, see Chapter 7.

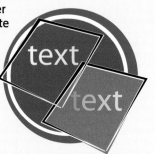

How can I give my text a neon look?

You can apply the Neon Glow filter to your text. This filter is under the Artistic submenu.

Create Warped Text

Elements' Warped Text feature lets you easily bend and distort layers of text. This can help you stylize your text to match the theme of your image.

Create Warped Text

1 In the Editor, click the **Horizontal Type** tool (T).

Note: For details about opening the Editor or opening palettes, see Chapter 1.

2 Click the text layer that you want to warp.

3 Click the **Create Warped Text** button (T).

The Warp Text dialog box appears.

4 Click here and then click a warp style.

⑤ Click to select an orientation for the warp effect (● changes to ○).

⑥ Adjust the Bend and Distortion values by clicking and dragging the sliders (▣).

The Bend and Distortion values determine how Elements applies the warp.

For all settings, a value of 0% means Elements does not apply that aspect of a warp.

⑦ Click **OK**.

Photoshop Elements warps the text.

You can still edit the format, color, and other characteristics of the type when you apply a warp.

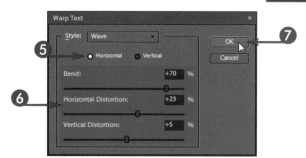

TIP

How do I unwarp text?

① Follow steps **1** to **3** in this section.

② In the Warp Text dialog box, click here and select **None**.

③ Click **OK**.

Your text unwarps.

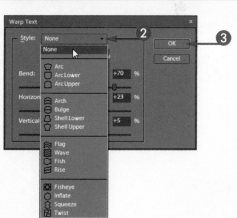

Create Beveled Text

You can give your text a raised look by adding a beveled effect. Elements offers several beveled options in the Effects palette.

For more information about Elements' effects, see Chapter 14.

Create Beveled Text

1 In the Editor, select a text layer.

Note: *For details about opening the Editor or opening palettes, see Chapter 1.*

2 In the Effects palette, click **Layer Styles** ().

Elements displays the bevel effects.

3 Click a bevel effect.

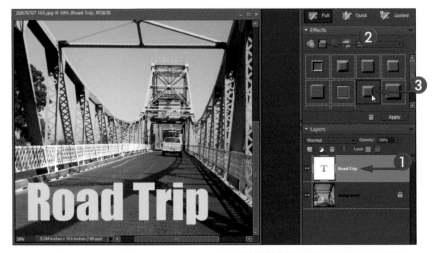

4 Click **Apply**.

Elements applies the effect to the text.

● Elements adds an icon to the layer to show that the layer includes an effect. You can double-click the icon to edit the effect.

You can cast a shadow behind your text to give the letters a 3-D look. Elements offers several shadow options in the Effects palette.

For more information about Elements' effects, see Chapter 14.

Add a Shadow to Text

① In the Editor, select a text layer.

Note: *For details about opening the Editor or opening palettes, see Chapter 1.*

② In the Effects palette, click **Layer Styles** (🔲).

③ Click here and select **Drop Shadows**.

Elements displays the Drop Shadow effects.

④ Click a shadow effect.

⑤ Click **Apply**.

Elements applies a shadow to the text.

● Elements adds an icon to the layer to show that the layer includes an effect.

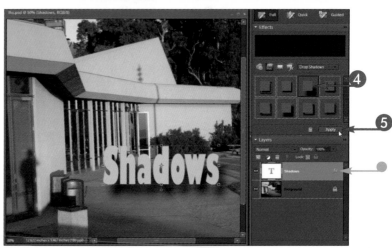

CHAPTER 14

Applying Styles and Effects

You can apply special effects to your images using Photoshop Elements' built-in styles and effects. The effects let you add shadows, glows, and a 3-D appearance to your art. You can also add special effects to your layers with Elements' layer styles.

Add a Drop Shadow to a Photo

You can apply a drop shadow to make your photo look like it is floating above the image canvas.

You can also apply a drop shadow to just a layer. See the section "Add a Drop Shadow to a Layer" for more information. Because this effect flattens the layers in your multilayer image, it is best to apply it last.

Add a Drop Shadow to a Photo

① In the Editor, open the Effects palette.

Note: For details about opening the Editor or opening palettes, see Chapter 1.

② Click the **Photo Effects** "button (▣).

③ Click here and then click **Frame**.

The frame effects appear.

4 Double-click the **Drop Shadow Frame** effect.

● Photoshop Elements duplicates the selected layer and applies the effect.

TIPS

What other shadow effects are there?

You can select a part of your image and then apply the **Recessed Frame** effect. This places a shadow along the inner edge of the selection, creating an effect that is the opposite of a drop-shadow effect.

How do I undo an effect?

Immediately after applying the effect, you can click **Edit** and then **Undo**, or click the **Undo** button ( ) in the Options bar. You can also undo an effect by using the Undo History palette. Click **Window** and then **Undo History** to access it.

You can add a drop shadow to a layer to give objects in your photo a 3-D look.

Add a Drop Shadow to a Layer

① In the Editor, open the Layers palette.

Note: *For details about opening the Editor or opening palettes, see Chapter 1.*

② Open the Effects palette.

③ Click the **Layer Styles** button (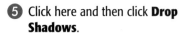).

④ Click the layer to which you want to add a drop shadow.

⑤ Click here and then click **Drop Shadows**.

The Drop Shadow styles appear.

6 Click a drop-shadow style.

Photoshop Elements applies the drop shadow to the layer.

7 Double-click the **Style** button (🔲) in the affected layer.

The Style Settings dialog box opens.

8 Click and drag the **Lighting Angle** dial to specify the direction of the shadowing.

9 Click and drag the Distance slider (🔲) to increase or decrease the distance of the shadow from your layer.

10 Click **OK**.

Photoshop Elements applies the style settings.

TIP

How can I add color shading to a layer using layer styles?

You can add color shading to a layer using the Photographic Effects styles.

1 Click a layer.

2 Open the Effects palette.

3 Click the **Layer Styles** button (🔲).

4 Click here and then click **Photographic Effects**.

5 Double-click an effect.

Photoshop Elements applies the shading.

Create a Vintage Photo

You can apply an effect that removes color and adds a wrinkled texture, creating the look of an older snapshot.

Create a Vintage Photo

1. In the Editor, open the Effects palette.

Note: For details about opening the Editor or opening palettes, see Chapter 1.

2. Click the **Photo Effects** button (▣).

3. Click here and then click **Vintage Photo**.

A Vintage Photo effect appears.

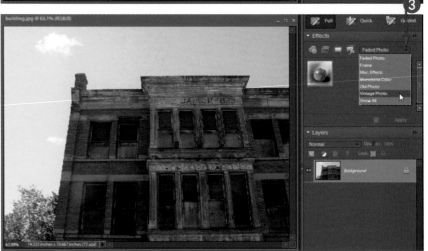

④ Double-click the effect.

● Photoshop Elements duplicates the selected layer and applies the effect.

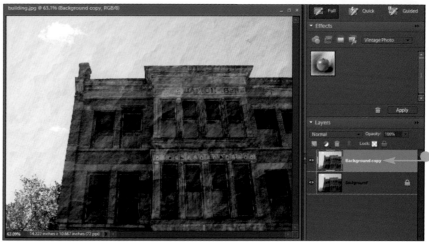

TIP

How can I partially fade the color in my photo?
You can give your photo a weathered appearance by applying one of the Faded Photo effects:

① In the Effects palette, click the **Photo Effects** button (▣).

② Click here and then click **Faded Photo**.

③ Double-click one of the Faded Photo effects.

The different effects apply fading to the right side, the top, and the middle of your photo.

Photoshop Elements fades the colors in your photo.

Add a Fancy Background

You can add a fancy background to your image with one of Elements' several texture effects.

Add a Fancy Background

1. In the Editor, open the Layers palette.

   Note: *For details about opening the Editor or opening palettes, see Chapter 1.*

2. Open the Effects palette.

3. Click the **Layer Styles** button (🔲).

4. Click the layer above which you want to add the fancy background.

5. Click here and then click **Patterns**.

   The pattern styles appear.

⑥ Double-click a style.

⑦ If you selected the Background layer in step 4, a dialog box appears asking if you want to make your background a normal layer. Click **OK** and then click **OK** again in the dialog box that follows.

Photoshop Elements applies a pattern to the selected layer, creating a background behind the other layers.

TIPS

How can I reduce the strength of an effect that I just applied?

In cases where the effect is applied to a duplicate layer, you can reduce the opacity of the new layer to lessen the effect. Reducing the opacity to less than 100% allows the original content underneath to show through.

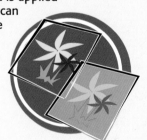

How can I customize the Effects palette?

Clicking Style menu arrows (▶▶) in the palette opens a menu that allows you to tailor the Effects palette to your liking. You can select different thumbnail sizes for each effect and display their names. Selecting **Styles and Effects Help** opens a Web browser with information about the different effects.

You can bevel a layer to give objects in your image a 3-D look. Bevel effects add shadowing to the edges of your layers.

Add Beveling to a Layer

① In the Editor, open the Layers palette.

Note: For details about opening the Editor or opening palettes, see Chapter 1.

② Open the Effects palette.

③ Click the layer to which you want to apply beveling.

In this example, a text layer is beveled.

Note: For more information about using text, see Chapter 13.

④ Click the **Layer Styles** button (▣).

⑤ Click here and then click **Bevels**.

Photoshop Elements displays the bevel styles.

6 Double-click a bevel style.

Photoshop Elements applies the beveling to the layer.

7 Double-click the **Style** button (*fx*) in the affected layer.

The Style Settings dialog box opens.

8 Click and drag the **Lighting Angle** dial to set the direction of the beveling.

9 Click and drag the slider (▢) to increase or decrease the bevel size.

● You can click to set the bevel direction (▢ changes to ✓).

10 Click **OK**.

Photoshop Elements applies the style settings.

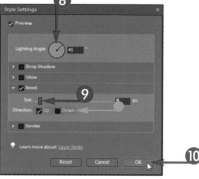

TIPS

When would I use the bevel style?
You may find this effect useful for creating 3-D buttons for Web pages. For example, to create such a 3-D button, you can apply beveling to a colored rectangle and then lay type over it. See Chapter 11 for details about drawing shapes.

How can I remove a style from a layer after I have applied it?
In the Layers palette, you can right-click the affected layer and then click **Clear Layer Style**. Photoshop Elements removes the style from the layer.

Add an Outer Glow to a Layer

The outer-glow style adds faint coloring to the outside edge of a layer, which can help highlight it.

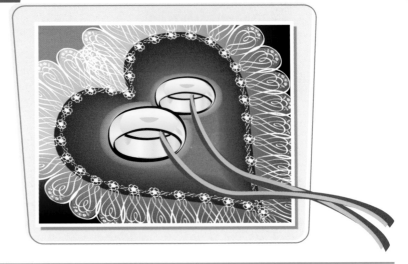

Add an Outer Glow to a Layer

1 In the Editor, open the Layers palette.

Note: *For details about opening the Editor or opening palettes, see Chapter 1.*

2 Open the Effects palette.

3 Click the layer to which you want to apply the outer glow.

4 Click the **Layer Styles** button (🔲).

5 Click here and then click **Outer Glows**.

Photoshop Elements displays the outer-glow styles.

6 Double-click an outer-glow style.

Photoshop Elements applies the outer glow to the layer.

7 Double-click the **Style** button (fx) in the affected layer.

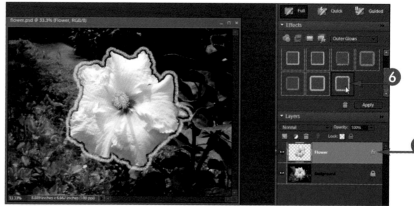

The Style Settings dialog box opens.

8 Click and drag the slider (▣) to increase or decrease the outer-glow size.

9 Click **OK**.

Photoshop Elements applies the style settings.

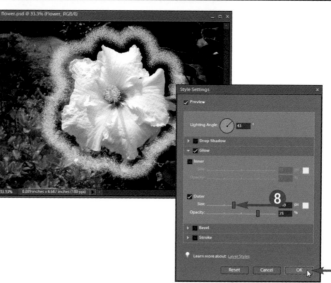

TIP

Can I add an inner glow to layer objects?
Yes. An inner glow adds color to the inside edge of a layer object. To add this effect:

1 Click a layer.

2 Open the Effects palette.

3 Click the **Layer Styles** button (▣).

4 Click here and then click **Inner Glows** from the menu that appears.

5 Double-click an inner-glow style.

Photoshop Elements applies the inner glow.

Add a Fancy Covering to a Layer

You can apply any of a variety of layer effects that can make a layer look as if it is covered in colorful metal or glass.

COVER WITH GLASS

1 In the Editor, open the Layers palette.

2 Open the Effects palette.

Note: For details about opening the Editor or opening palettes, see Chapter 1.

3 Click the layer that you want to cover.

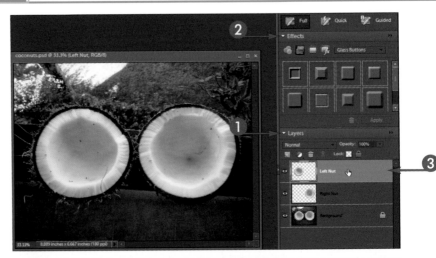

4 Click the **Layer Styles** button (▣).

5 Click here and then click **Glass Buttons**.

Photoshop Elements displays a number of glass styles.

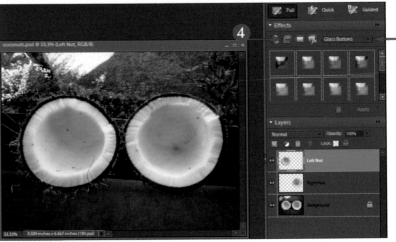

6 Double-click a style.

Photoshop Elements applies the style to the layer.

COVER WITH METAL

1 Click the layer that you want to cover.

2 Click here and then click **Complex**.

Photoshop Elements displays various styles.

3 Double-click the **Diamond Plate** style.

Photoshop Elements applies the style to the layer.

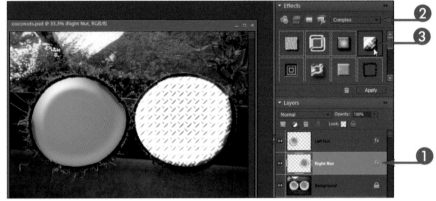

 TIP

Is there another way to change how styles affect my layers?

Yes. You can change the intensity of your styles by scaling them.

1 Click a layer.

2 Click **Layer**.

3 Click **Layer Style**.

4 Click **Scale Effects**.

5 In the Scale Layer Effects dialog box, type a value to scale the effects from 1% to 1000%.

6 Click **OK**.

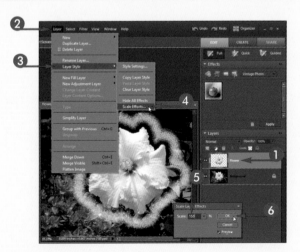

Add a Watermark

Photoshop Elements can automatically add watermarks to a collection of photos. Watermarks are semi-opaque words or designs overlaid on images to signify ownership and discourage illegal use.

Before you can begin, you need to create a source folder and a destination folder for your images. To work with folders, see your operating system's documentation.

Add a Watermark

① Place the images to which you want to add watermarks into a source folder.

② Create an empty destination folder in which to save your watermarked files.

③ In the Elements Editor, click **File**.

④ Click **Process Multiple Files**.

The Process Multiple Files dialog box opens.

⑤ Click **Browse**.

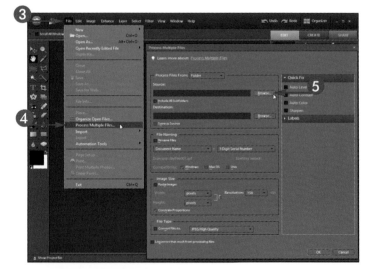

The Browse for Folder dialog box opens.

⑥ Click the folder containing your images.

⑦ Click **OK**.

⑧ Click **Browse** and repeat steps **6** and **7** for the destination folder.

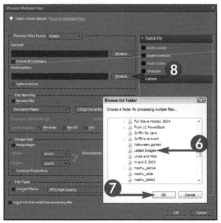

⑨ Click here to open the Labels palette (▶ changes to ▼).

⑩ Click here and then select **Watermark**.

⑪ Type your watermark text.

⑫ Select a position, font, and size for the text.

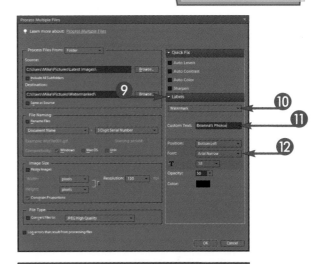

⑬ Click here and specify an opacity from 1 to 100. The lower the opacity, the more transparent the watermark will be.

⑭ Click the color box and select a watermark color.

You may want to select a color that contrasts with the colors in your photo.

⑮ Click **OK**.

Photoshop Elements adds watermarks to the photos in the source folder and saves them in the destination folder.

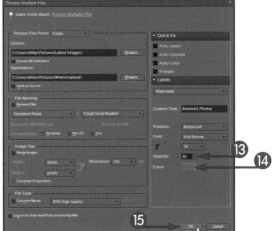

TIPS

How can I automatically add captions to my photos?

In the Process Multiple Files dialog box, you can select **Caption** under the top menu in the Labels palette. With Caption chosen, Elements applies text that is associated with the photo to the top of the photo. Similar to applying a watermark, you can specify the positioning, font, size, opacity, and color of the caption.

What kinds of captions can I add to my photos?

You can add the file name, date modified, and description as a caption. You can add this information by itself — for example, just the file name — or in combination by clicking one or more options (■ changes to ✓) in the Process Multiple Files dialog box.

Presenting Photos Creatively

You can use photos that you have edited in Photoshop Elements in a variety of creative projects. Some of the projects, such as the greeting card and photo collage, can be output on your printer. Others, such as PhotoStamps, must be purchased online through Adobe Photoshop Services. This chapter introduces you to some of the more interesting creative projects in Elements.

Create a Slide Show

The Create feature in Organizer lets you make a variety of projects using the photos in your Organizer catalog. For example, you can create slide shows and share them with others, or turn your photos into album pages, calendars, and even Web galleries.

Slide shows are easy to share with others by copying the finished file onto a disk, sending it to your TV, or e-mailing it.

Create a Slide Show

① In the Organizer, Ctrl-click the images you want to display in your slide show.

Note: For details about using the Organizer, see Chapter 3.

② Click **Create**.

③ Click **Slide Show**.

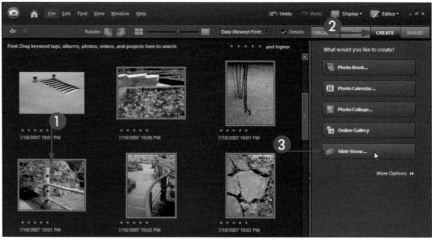

The Slide Show Preferences dialog box appears.

④ Select a duration, transition, and other options.

⑤ Specify the quality of the preview photos. Choosing a lower quality results in a smaller file size.

⑥ Click **OK**.

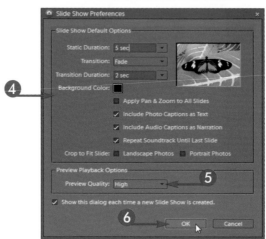

The Slide Show Editor dialog box opens.

● To add more photos to your slide show, you can click **Add Media**.

● Elements displays icons for the slides and transitions along the bottom of the Slide Show Editor.

⑦ Click a slide to which you want to add text.

⑧ Click **Add Text**.

The Edit Text dialog box appears.

⑨ Type your text.

⑩ Click **OK**.

Elements adds the text to the selected slide.

The text properties appear.

⑪ Choose formatting options for your text.

⑫ Repeat steps **7** to **11** for the other slides in your slide show.

TIPS

How do I rearrange the photos in my slide show?

In the Slide Show Editor dialog box, you can click and drag the photo thumbnails at the bottom to change their order in the slide show. To remove a slide entirely, right-click it and click **Delete Slide**. If you have a lot of slides, you can click **Quick Reorder** to view and rearrange them in a larger window.

How do I add music to my slide show?

To add music or narration to a slide show, click **Add Media** and then one of the audio options in the Slide Show Editor. Or you can click the audio timeline located below the slide and transition thumbnails. You can add an audio file that plays in the background while the slide show runs. Organizer supports MP3, WAV, and WMA audio file formats. You can click **Fit Slides To Audio** located below the Play button (▶) to sync your slide show with the audio.

continued

When creating a slide show, you can control the transition effects and slide duration, and even set the show to loop continuously. Transition effects control how one slide flows to the next.

Organizer saves your slide show as either a WMV file or a PDF file. The WMV format can be viewed with Windows Media Player, and a PDF can be viewed using Adobe Acrobat Reader.

Create a Slide Show *(continued)*

⑬ If the Extras panel is closed, click **Extras** to open it.

The Extras panel includes clip art that you can use to decorate your slides.

⑭ Click a slide to which you want to add clip art.

⑮ Click and drag the clip art to the slide.

You can click and drag the clip art to reposition it.

● Choose options here to resize or recolor the clip art.

⑯ Click a transition icon between the slides.

The transition properties appear.

⑰ Click here to select a transition duration.

⑱ Click here to select a transition style.

You can repeat steps **16** to **18** for other transitions.

19 Click the **Play** button to preview your slide show (► changes to ❚❚).

Elements cycles through the slides.

You can click the **Pause** button (❚❚) to pause the preview.

● You can click **Full Screen Preview** to preview the slide show at full size

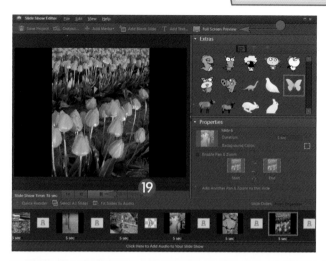

20 Click **Save Project**.

A window opens asking you to a name your slide show.

21 Type a name.

22 Click **Save**.

Photoshop Elements saves your slide show to the Organizer.

23 Click here to close the Slide Show editor and return to the Organizer.

● You can click **Output** to save the slide show as a PDF file or movie, or burn it to a CD or DVD.

TIP

How do I add a title page to my slide show?

1 Click a slide thumbnail. Your title page will be inserted after this slide.

2 Click **Add Blank Slide**.

● Elements adds a blank slide to your slide show.

3 Click **Add Text**.

4 In the dialog box that appears, type a title for your page.

5 Click **OK**.

You can click and drag the new title page to reposition it (for example, to before the first slide in your slide show).

Create an Online Photo Gallery

You can have Photoshop Elements create a photo gallery Web site that showcases your images. Elements not only sizes and optimizes your image files for the site, but also creates the Web pages that display the images and links those pages together.

① In the Organizer, Ctrl-click the images you want to display in your gallery.

Note: *For details about using the Organizer, see Chapter 3.*

If you do not select any photos, you can add them in step 4.

② Click **Create**.

③ Click **Online Gallery**.

The Online Gallery window appears.

④ Add more images to your gallery by clicking them in the Photo Browser and clicking plus (➕).

● To remove an item from the gallery, click it and then click minus (➖).

⑤ Click **Next**.

6 Click here and select a category.

Elements displays templates from the category.

7 Select a template.

Note: *The following steps may differ depending on the category and template you selected in steps* ***6*** *and* ***7***.

8 Click **Next**.

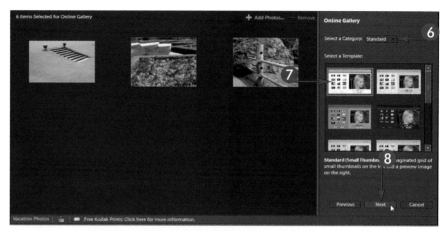

Photoshop Elements builds your gallery.

9 Type a title and other information here to add it to your gallery.

10 Click here to choose the slide duration and transition effect.

11 Click here to choose a connection type. Elements can optimize the file sizes in the gallery for fast or slow online connections.

TIPS

How can I label the photos in my photo gallery?

At the bottom of the Online Gallery options, you can select **Show Captions** or **Show File Names** (■ changes to ✓) to label the photos in your online gallery. In most of the templates, Elements applies the labels below your photos. For more about adding captions to your photos, see Chapter 3.

How does the e-mail address appear in my gallery?

You can add an e-mail address in step **9**. How the e-mail address appears depends on the gallery template you chose. In most of the standard templates, the e-mail address is associated with your name, which you can also add in step **9**; clicking your name opens a new e-mail message on the viewer's computer.

continued

When you create a Web photo gallery, you specify a template that determines the colors and imagery included in the gallery. You can customize the colors and add a title, your name, and other descriptive information. During the last step, you can upload your photos to a Web server, if you have access to one.

⑫ Click here to choose a background color for the main window.

The Color Picker dialog box opens.

⑬ Click a color.

⑭ Click **OK**.

⑮ Repeat steps **12** to **14** for the other color options.

● You can click and drag the sliders to adjust the border and button opacity.

● You can customize the appearance of the title and menu bars here.

⑯ Click **Next**.

⑰ Type a name for your gallery.

⑱ Click **Browse**.

The Browse For Folder dialog box opens.

⑲ Click the destination for your new gallery folder.

⑳ Click **OK**.

● The folder appears in the Save To field. Your gallery will be saved in a subfolder with the name from step **17**.

㉑ Click **Next**.

Photoshop Elements saves your gallery to the Organizer.

You can test your gallery by clicking the thumbnails and controls.

㉒ Click **My FTP** to put the gallery on a Web server using File Transfer Protocol.

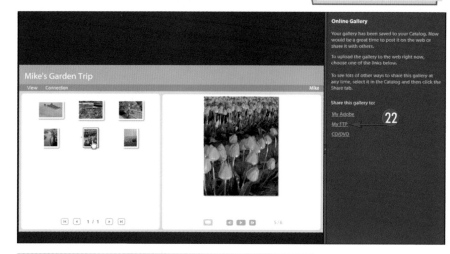

The Share Photo Gallery to My FTP dialog box opens.

㉓ Type a server address.

㉔ Type your server login information.

Your Internet service provider can give you information about your server address and login information.

● You can click here to test your connection before uploading.

㉕ Click here to upload your online gallery files to the server.

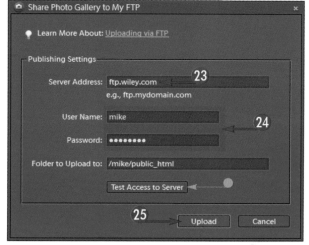

How do I put my online photo gallery on a CD or DVD?

In step **22**, you can click **CD/DVD** to save your gallery to a CD or DVD. A Make CD or DVD dialog box appears, allowing you to select a CD or DVD drive on your computer. Make sure a blank disc is in the drive, and click **OK**. Elements creates a gallery CD or DVD that can automatically start when you insert the disc into a computer.

How do I view my online photo gallery in a regular Web browser?

You can launch your Web browser and then open the index.html file located in the folder you specified in step 17. You can typically click **File** and then **Open** to open a file in your browser. The index.html file represents the home page of your online photo gallery.

Photoshop Elements lets you combine photos into a set of pages, which it calls a collage. You can customize the appearance of the photos and add artwork to the pages.

Create a Collage

① In the Organizer, Ctrl-click the images you want to include in your collage.

Note: *For details about using the Organizer, see Chapter 3.*

② Click **Create**.

③ Click **Photo Collage**.

The Editor opens and displays your images in the Photo Bin.

④ Click here and choose a page size for your collage.

● You can choose a theme for your collage.

⑤ Choose a layout for your collage.

● Elements displays a preview of the layout.

⑥ Click **Done**.

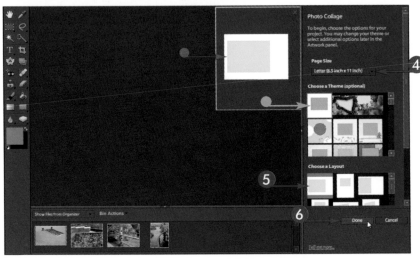

Elements creates a collage using the photos you selected.

To reposition your photo, click and drag inside it.

● To resize your photo, click and drag a corner handle.

● To crop your photo, click and drag a side handle.

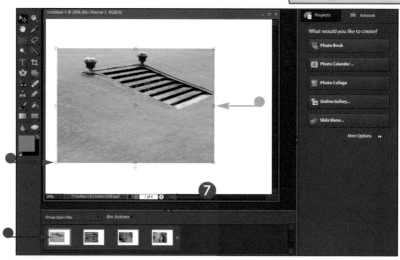

⑦ Click the **Next** button (▶) to view and edit the next photo.

● You can also click a page in the Photo Bin to go directly to that page.

⑧ Click **File**.

⑨ Click **Save**.

The Save As window opens.

⑩ Choose a destination folder.

⑪ Type a file name.

⑫ Click to select **Include in the Organizer** (■ changes to ✓) to add your collage to the Organizer.

⑬ Click **Save**.

Photoshop Elements saves your collage.

TIPS

How do I add text or artwork to my collage?

At the top of the Photo Collage panel, click **Artwork**. You can select from options to add backgrounds, frames, text, and other features to your collage pages. To add a feature, click and drag it to the page.

How can I create a hardcover book featuring my photos?

The Photo Book feature in Elements enables you to design a custom book with one or more of your photos on each page. Similar to the collage, you can choose a theme and layout for the book pages. You also choose a photo to appear on the initial title page. You can order a hardcover version of the book through Adobe Photoshop Services. To start creating such a book from the Organizer, click the **Create** tab and then click **Photo Book**.

You can design a printable greeting card using one of your Photoshop Elements photos. Elements lets you decorate your card with a variety of border styles and photo layouts. You can also add custom text.

Photoshop Elements' greeting card is more like a postcard than a foldable card; this feature creates a single image that you can print out.

Create a Greeting Card

1 In the Editor, open an image to use in your greeting card.

Note: For details about opening the Editor or opening an image, see Chapter 1.

2 Click **Create**.

3 Click **More Options**.

4 Click **Greeting Card**.

Alternatively, you can select **CD Jacket**, **DVD Jacket**, or **CD/DVD Label** to create other projects. The steps you use to create those projects are similar to those for the greeting card.

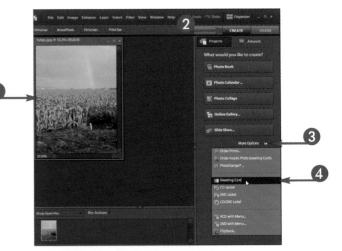

The Greeting Card options appear.

5 Click here to select a page size.

6 Click a theme.

● A pop-up preview of the theme appears.

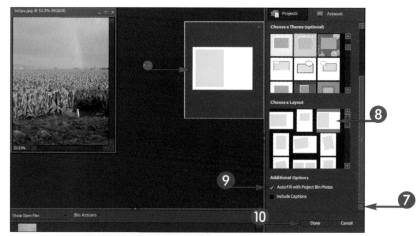

7 Click here to scroll down and view the other options.

8 Click a layout option.

● A pop-up preview of the layout appears.

9 Click to select **Auto-Fill** to add the open photo to your card automatically (▊ changes to ✔).

10 Click **Done**.

Elements displays the greeting card in a new image window.

11 To save the greeting card, click **File** and then **Save**.

Note: For more about saving, see Chapter 2. To print the card, see Chapter 16.

How do I add text to my greeting card?
You can personalize your greeting card by adding text. After completing step **10**, follow these steps:

1 Click **Artwork**.

2 Click here and then select **Text**.

3 Click a type style and drag it onto the greeting card.

4 Type your text and then press `Enter`.

5 In the bounding box, click the handles to change the size of the text. You can click and drag inside the text to reposition it.

6 Click ✔ to commit your changes.

Create a Flipbook

You can take a sequence of action photos and turn them into a flipbook, which is similar to a short movie. You can specify the frame rate of the movie as well as the dimensions.

① In the Organizer, **Ctrl**-click to select the photos you want to include in your flipbook.

Note: For details about using the Organizer, see Chapter 3.

② Click **Create**.

③ Click **More Options**.

④ Click **Flipbook**.

The Flipbook dialog box appears.

⑤ Type a playback speed of 1 to 30 fps. *Fps* stands for frames per second.

● You can also click and drag the slider (🔘) to set a playback speed.

● Your photos are ordered as they were in the Organizer. You can click to select this option (⬛ changes to ☑) to reverse the order.

6 Choose an output setting based on how the flipbook will be viewed. The setting determines the dimensions of the movie.

● You can click **Details** for an explanation of the current setting.

7 Click the **Play** button (▶) to preview your flipbook.

8 Click **Output**.

The Save Flip Book as WMV dialog box appears.

9 Type a file name for your flipbook.

● Only Windows Media File type is supported.

10 Click here to specify where the flipbook should be saved.

11 Click **Save**.

Photoshop Elements saves the flipbook.

The flipbook is also added to the Organizer.

 TIP

What are my options for previewing a flipbook?
Besides clicking the **Play** button (▶) to play the flipbook, you can do the following:

● Click and drag the slider (◻) to the left and right to cycle back and forth through the flipbook photos.

● Click the **Previous** button (◀) to go to the previous photo.

● Click the **Next** button (▶) to go to the next photo.

● Click to deselect **Loop Preview** (✓ changes to ◼) to stop the preview from looping.

Create PhotoStamps

You can turn an image into U.S. Postal Service–approved stamps using the PhotoStamps feature. After you upload the photo you want displayed on the stamp to the service, you can customize the stamp and then purchase a set.

Create PhotoStamps

① From the Organizer, click the photo you want to use in your stamps.

Note: *For details about using the Organizer, see Chapter 3.*

You can `Ctrl`-click to select multiple photos.

② Click **More Options**.

③ Click **PhotoStamps**.

④ In the PhotoStamps window that appears, click **Upload My Photos**.

Photoshop Elements uploads the photo to the PhotoStamps Web site.

⑤ In the confirmation window that appears, click **Continue**.

The Adobe Photoshop Services page opens in a browser window.

⑥ Click **Create Product** beneath your photo.

7 In the Image Details window that appears, click **PhotoStamps**.

The Customize Your PhotoStamps window appears.

8 Click options to customize your stamps.

You can zoom into or out of your photo, rotate it, add a border, or change the color of the postage amount.

9 Click **Continue**.

Your stamps are added to your shopping cart.

On the pages that follow, you can enter payment and shipping information to purchase the stamps.

How can I order prints of my Photoshop Elements photos?

You can order prints of your photos by clicking the **Create** tab, **More Options**, and then **Order Prints**. A window appears that enables you to create an account with the Kodak EasyShare Gallery service and order prints. You specify the size of the prints and have the option of sending them to multiple recipients.

How can I order greeting cards that feature my Photoshop Elements photos?

You can order custom greeting cards by clicking the **Create** tab, **More Options**, and then **Order Kodak Photo Greeting Cards**. A window appears that enables you to create an account with the Kodak EasyShare Gallery service and order greeting cards. This is separate from the Photoshop Elements greeting card feature covered in the section "Create a Greeting Card."

Create a Photo Panorama

You can use the Photomerge feature in Photoshop Elements to stitch several images together into a single panoramic image. This enables you to capture more scenery than is usually possible in a regular photograph.

Create a Photo Panorama

1 In the Editor, click **File**.

Note: For details about opening the Editor, see Chapter 1.

2 Click **New**.

3 Click **Photomerge Panorama**.

The Photomerge dialog box appears.

4 Click **Interactive Layout** (⬤ changes to ⭕).

5 Click **Browse**.

The Open dialog box appears.

6 Click here and select the folder that contains the images you want to merge.

7 Ctrl-click the images you want to merge into a panoramic image.

8 Click **OK**.

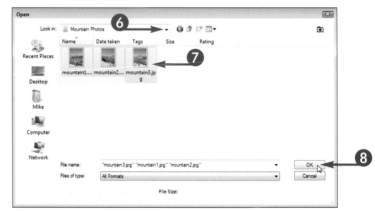

● The file names of the images appear in the Source Files list.

9 Click **OK** to build the panoramic image.

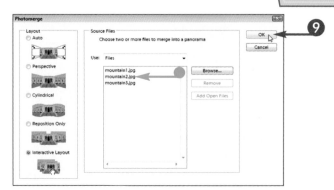

● Photoshop Elements attempts to merge the images into a single panoramic image.

● Thumbnails of the images that Photoshop Elements cannot merge appear in a lightbox area.

● You can click and drag the **Zoom** tool (🔍) to zoom the panoramic image in and out.

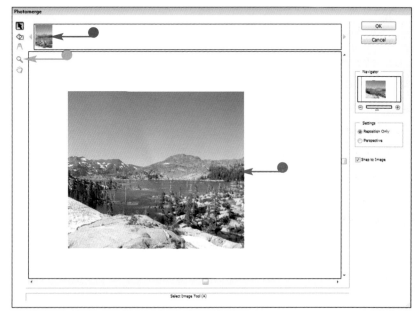

TIP

What are the different Photomerge layout options?
You can select alternative layout options in step **4** to determine how your panoramic images are combined:

● **Auto**: Photomerge analyzes your images and chooses the best layout (Perspective or Cylindrical) automatically.

● **Perspective**: One of the middle images is selected as a reference image. Then Photomerge stretches the images to the sides of it to merge them.

● **Cylindrical**: Photomerge corrects for the distortion that can occur with the Perspective layout by displaying the images as if on an unfolded cylinder. This layout works well for very wide panoramas.

● **Reposition** Only: Photomerge aligns the images to match their content but does not distort the images.

● **Interactive Layout**: This layout enables you to align your images manually by clicking and dragging. Photomerge then merges the content.

continued

The Photomerge dialog box
enables you to interactively align
the images that make up your
panorama.

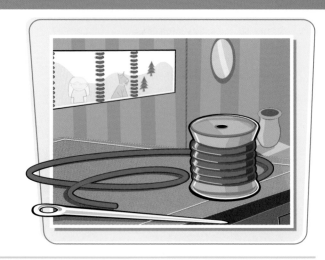

Create a Photo Panorama *(continued)*

⑩ Click the **Select Image** tool (⬚).

⑪ Click and drag an image from the
lightbox to the work area.

⑫ Place the image so that it lines up with
its neighboring image in the panorama.

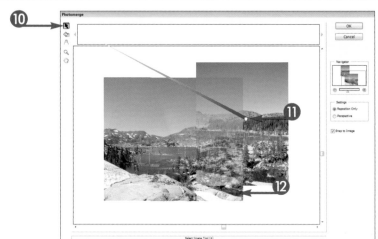

● If you select **Snap to Image**
(⬛ changes to ✅), Photoshop
Elements tries to merge the image
edges after you click and drag.

● You can use the **Move View** tool (🖐)
to adjust the placement of the entire
panoramic image inside the main
window.

⑬ Repeat steps **10** to **12** for any other
images in the lightbox so that they
overlap and match one another.

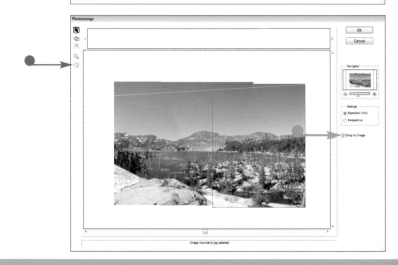

● You can click the **Rotate Image** tool ( ) and then click and drag with it to align image seams that are not level with one another.

⑭ Click **OK**.

Photoshop Elements merges the images and opens the panorama in a new image window.

● Elements places parts of each photo in their own layers in the Layers palette.

● You can crop the panorama to remove any white space around the edges.

Note: To save the panorama, see Chapter 2. See Chapter 8 for more about cropping.

TIP

How can I create photos that merge successfully?
To merge photos successfully, you need to align and overlap the photos. Here are a few hints. For more tips, see the Photoshop Elements Help documentation.

● Use a tripod to keep your photos level with one another.

● Experiment with the Perspective setting in the Photomerge dialog box. This setting can be helpful if you use a tripod to shoot your photos.

● Refrain from using lenses, such as fisheye lenses, that distort your photos.

● Shoot your photos so they overlap at least 30 percent.

CHAPTER 16

Saving and Sharing Your Work

Photoshop Elements lets you save your images in different file formats for use on the Web. You can also share your photos by e-mailing them, or print them out to put in physical photo albums. For safekeeping, you can export your photos to a separate folder on your computer or back them up to a CD or DVD.

You can save a file in the JPEG — Joint Photographic Experts Group — format and publish it on the Web. JPEG is the preferred Web format for saving photographic images.

Photoshop Elements saves JPEG images at 72 dpi.

Save a JPEG for the Web

① In the Editor, click **File**.

Note: For details about opening the Editor, see Chapter 1.

② Click **Save for Web**.

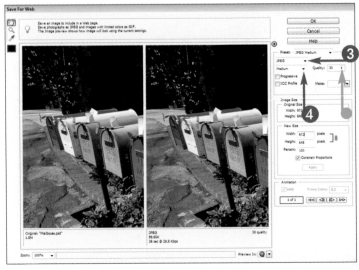

The Save For Web dialog box appears.

Your original image is displayed on the left and a preview of the JPEG version is on the right.

③ Click here and select **JPEG**.

④ Click here and select a quality setting.

● Alternatively, you can select a numeric quality setting from **0** (low quality) to **100** (high quality).

The higher the quality, the larger the resulting file size.

⑤ Check that the file quality and size are acceptable in the preview window.

● You can resize the resulting image by typing dimensions or a percentage and then clicking **Apply**.

⑥ Click **OK**.

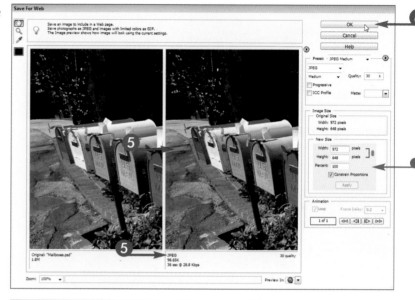

The Save Optimized As dialog box appears.

⑦ Click here and select a folder in which to save the file.

⑧ Type a file name. Photoshop Elements automatically assigns a .jpg extension if you do not specify an extension.

⑨ Click **Save**.

The original image file remains open.

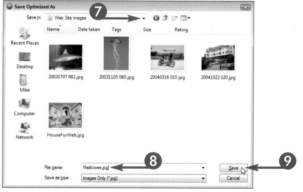

TIPS

What is image compression?

Image compression involves using mathematical techniques to reduce the amount of information required to describe an image. This results in smaller file sizes, which is important when transmitting information on the Web. Some compression schemes, such as JPEG, reduce image quality somewhat, but the loss is usually negligible compared to the savings in file size.

How can I adjust the view of my image in the Save For Web dialog box?

You can use the Hand tool (🖐) in the upper-left corner to shift the position of your image in the Save For Web dialog box or use the Zoom tool (🔍) to zoom in or out.

Save a GIF for the Web

You can save an image as a GIF — Graphics Interchange Format — file and publish it on the Web. The GIF format is good for saving illustrations that have a lot of solid color. The format supports a maximum of 256 colors.

Photoshop Elements saves GIF images at 72 dpi. Unlike JPEG images, GIF images can include transparency.

Save a GIF for the Web

1 In the Editor, click **File**.

Note: For details about opening the Editor, see Chapter 1.

2 Click **Save for Web**.

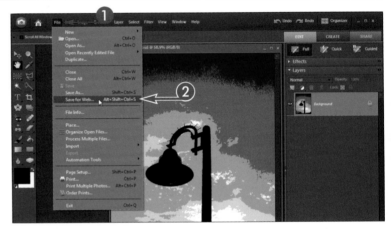

The Save For Web dialog box appears.

3 Click here and select **GIF**.

4 Click here and select the number of colors to include in the image.

GIF allows a maximum of 256 colors.

● You can click here to choose the method Elements uses to select the GIF colors.

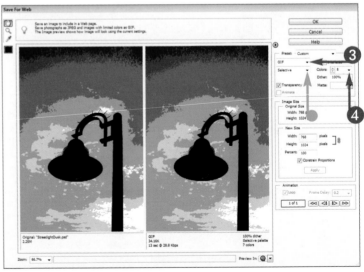

⑤ Check that the file quality and size are acceptable in the preview window.

● You can resize the resulting image by typing dimensions or a percentage and then clicking **Apply**.

● Selecting **Transparency** (changes to ✓) ensures that any transparent areas of your image remain that way in your final GIF image.

⑥ Click **OK**.

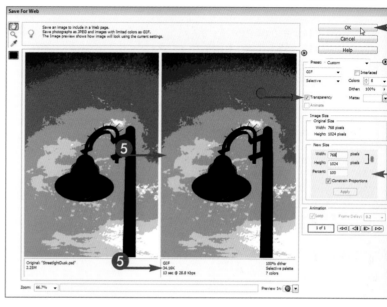

The Save Optimized As dialog box appears.

⑦ Click here and select a folder in which to save the file.

⑧ Type a file name. Photoshop Elements automatically assigns a .gif extension if you do not specify an extension.

⑨ Click **Save**.

The original image file remains open.

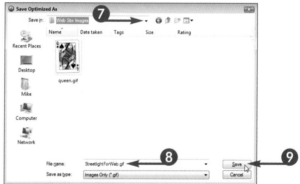

 TIPS

How do I minimize the file sizes of my GIF images?

The most important factor in creating small GIFs is limiting the number of colors in the final image. GIF files are limited to 256 colors or fewer. In images that have just a few solid colors, you can often reduce the total number of colors to 16 or even 8 without any noticeable reduction in quality. See step **4** in this section to set the number of colors in your GIF images.

How can I use GIF transparency in my Web images?

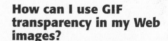

GIF images that include transparency allow the background of a Web page to show through. Transparent GIFs enable you to add non-rectangular elements to your Web projects. Because Background layers cannot contain transparent pixels, you need to work with layers other than the Background layer to create transparent GIFs. See Chapter 7 for more about layers.

Save a PNG for the Web

You can save an image as a
PNG — Portable Network
Graphics — file and publish
it on the Web.

PNG was devised as a higher-quality
alternative to GIF. Unlike GIF, PNG can
support more than 256 colors. However, it
is not as universally supported as GIF and
JPEG are by Web browsers.

Save a PNG for the Web

① In the Editor, click **File**.

Note: For details about opening the Editor, see Chapter 1.

② Click **Save for Web**.

The Save For Web dialog box appears.

③ Click here and select **PNG-8** or
PNG-24.

*Note: See the tip on the opposite page for details about
the different PNG settings.*

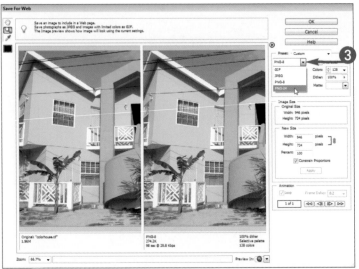

④ Check that the file quality and size are acceptable in the preview window.

● You can resize the resulting image by typing dimensions or a percentage and then clicking **Apply**.

● Selecting **Transparency** (■ changes to ✓) ensures that any transparent areas of your image remain that way in your final PNG image.

⑤ Click **OK**.

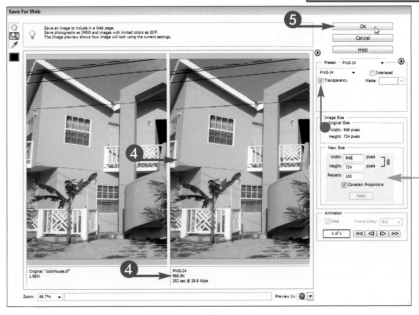

⑥ Click here and select a folder in which to save the file.

⑦ Type a file name. Photoshop Elements automatically assigns a .png extension if you do not specify an extension.

⑧ Click **Save**.

The original image file remains open.

What is the difference between the PNG-8 and PNG-24 settings?

PNG-8 stands for PNG 8-bit. With it, you can limit the number of colors in the final PNG image and thereby decrease the resulting file size. Similar to GIF, PNG-8 can include a maximum of 256 colors. PNG-24 stands for PNG 24-bit. This format includes a wider range of colors than 8-bit and leads to better image quality, but generally results in much larger file sizes.

How does the PNG format support transparency?

Like GIF files, PNG files can include transparency. But unlike GIFs, the PNG format supports a more advanced feature called alpha-channel transparency, which allows a background behind an image to show through partially. You can add partial transparency to your image by decreasing the opacity of a layer. For more information about layers and opacity, see Chapter 7.

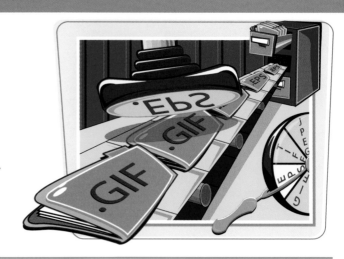

You can quickly and easily convert images from one file type to another in Photoshop Elements using the Process Multiple Files feature. This makes it easy to convert a collection of PSD files to the JPEG format for sending by e-mail or posting on the Web.

Convert File Types

1 Place the images that you want to convert in a folder.

Note: To work with folders, see your operating system's documentation.

2 In the Editor, click **File**.

Note: For details about opening the Editor, see Chapter 1.

3 Click **Process Multiple Files**.

The Process Multiple Files dialog box appears.

4 Click **Browse**.

The Browse for Folder dialog box appears.

5 Click here to open folders on your computer (⊳ changes to ▽).

6 Click the folder containing your images.

7 Click **OK**.

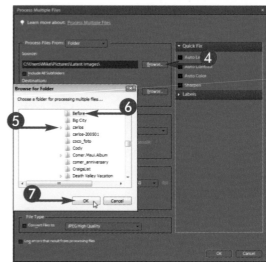

⑧ Click **Browse** and repeat steps **5** to **7** to specify the folder where you want your processed images to be saved.

⬤ You can optionally select **Resize Images** (■ changes to ☑) and type a new width and height, and Photoshop Elements resizes the images before saving.

Note: For more about resizing images, see Chapter 4.

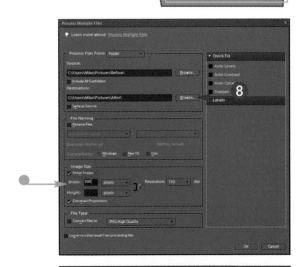

⑨ Click to select **Convert Files to** (■ changes to ☑).

⑩ Click here and select a file format to convert to.

⑪ Click **OK**.

Photoshop Elements processes the images and saves them in the destination folder.

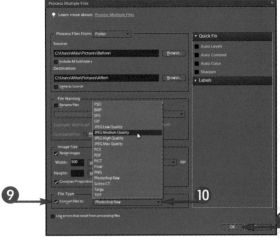

TIPS

How can I automatically fix color and lighting problems in my converted photos?

There are automatic optimization settings under the Quick Fix heading in the Process Multiple Files dialog box. You can select them to have Photoshop Elements improve the contrast and color of your photos before they are converted. See Chapter 9 for more on contrast and other lighting topics. See Chapter 10 for more on optimizing the colors in your photos.

How can I quickly add labels to my converted photos?

Under the Labels heading in the Process Multiple Files dialog box, there are tools for adding captions and watermarks to your converted photos. You can automatically add file name, description, and date information as captions and specify the size and style of the caption font. For information about adding watermarks, see Chapter 14.

E-mail Images with Photo Mail

You can embed your images in an e-mail message and send them to others using Elements' Photo Mail feature. With Photo Mail, you can select custom stationery that lets you insert colors, graphics, and captions next to your images.

This feature requires that you already have an e-mail program, such as Microsoft Outlook, set up on your computer. Photoshop Elements does not come with e-mail capability.

E-mail Images with Photo Mail

① In the Organizer, click **Share**.

Note: *For details about using the Organizer, see Chapter 3.*

② Click **Photo Mail**.

Note: *Photoshop Elements may display a window asking you to choose your e-mail client. If so, choose the software with which you prefer to send e-mail and click **Continue**.*

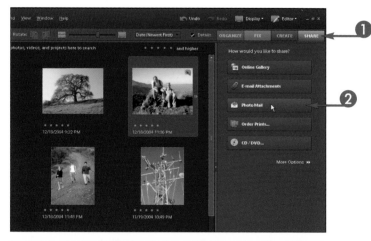

The Photo Mail pane opens.

③ Click and drag images you want to mail from the main Organizer window into the Photo Mail pane.

● Photoshop Elements totals the file sizes and estimates how long they will take to send.

④ Click **Next**.

5 Type a message to accompany your images.

6 Click the **Contact Book** button () to define your recipient.

The Contact Book dialog box appears.

7 Click **New Contact**.

The New Contact dialog box appears.

8 Type the contact details for your recipient.

9 Type an e-mail address for your recipient.

10 Click **OK**.

● The recipient appears in the Contact Book.

11 Click **OK** in the Contact Book dialog box.

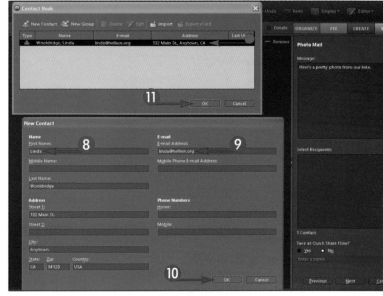

continued

TIPS

Can I send my images as e-mail attachments?

If you want to send your photos as plain e-mail attachments rather than as embedded items in an e-mail message, click the **E-mail Attachments** option in the Organizer's Share pane. Sending attachments is similar to sending Photo Mail but without the steps where you select stationery and a layout.

How can I keep the file sizes of my images small when e-mailing them?

If you are worried about the file sizes of your images when e-mailing, choose the **E-mail Attachments** option rather than the Photo Mail option in the Organizer's Share pane. In the E-mail Attachments options, you can adjust both the dimensions of your photos and the JPEG compression that is applied prior to sending.

Photo Mail includes more than 50 stationery designs that you can apply to the photos you e-mail. You can select stationery with animal, seasonal, or party themes. Elements embeds your images and the stationery into the e-mail message using HTML.

The new contact appears in the Select Recipients list.

⑫ Click to select each recipient (■ changes to ✔).

⑬ Click **Next**.

The Stationery & Layouts Wizard window appears with the Choose a Stationery options.

● You can click a category to open stationery options.

⑭ Click a stationery with which to style your e-mail.

● You can click text inside the stationery design to caption your images.

⑮ Click **Next Step**.

The Customize the Layout options appear.

⑯ Click the layout options to organize and size your images.

● You can optionally customize your text.

● You can also customize the borders around your images.

⑰ Click **Next**.

Photoshop Elements opens a new message in your e-mail client software.

● The recipient is added to the To field.

● Your message text, layout design, and images are included in the body of the message.

Note: For more information about sending your message, see the documentation for your e-mail application.

How do I use the Quick Share feature?
You can set up a Quick Share item for recipients with whom you share photos regularly.

① In the Photo Mail pane, under Save as Quick Share Flow, click to select **Yes** (● changes to ○).

② Type a shortcut name for the Quick Share.

③ Finish the steps for sending Photo Mail.

In the Share pane in the Organizer, your recipient now appears in the Quick Share list.

④ To send photos, click and drag the images to the Quick Share list.

⑤ Click **E-mail** to finish sharing the photos.

You can print your Photoshop Elements images to create hard copies of your work. You can then add your photos to a physical photo album.

Print a Photo

① In the Editor, make sure the layers you want to print are visible.

Note: For details about opening the Editor, see Chapter 1.

Note: The Layer Visibility icon (👁) means that a layer is visible. To read more about layers, see Chapter 7.

② Click **File**.

③ Click **Print**.

The Print dialog box appears.

④ Type a percentage in the Scale box to shrink or enlarge the image.

⑤ To resize the image, select the **Show Bounding Box** option (☐ changes to ☑).

⑥ Deselect **Center Image** to allow repositioning of the image (☑ changes to ☐).

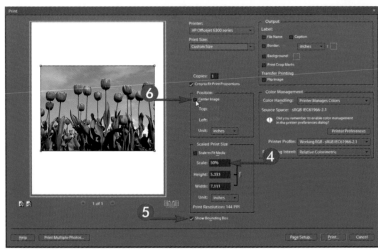

⑦ Click and drag in the image window to reposition the image on the page.

● You can position your image precisely by typing values in the Top and Left fields.

● You can click and drag the handles on the image corners to scale the image by hand.

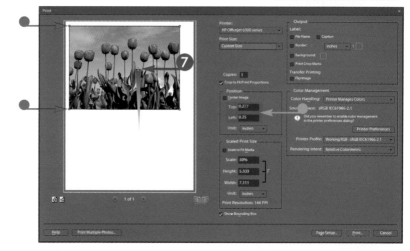

⑧ Click here and choose a printer.

⑨ Type the number of copies to print.

⑩ Click **Print**.

A smaller Print dialog box appears.

● You can click **Show Printer Preferences** to set printer-specific options.

⑪ Click **Print** to print the image.

TIPS

What is the difference between portrait and landscape orientation?

Portrait, which is the default orientation for most printers, prints with the long edge of the page oriented vertically. A standard 8.5-x-11-inch sheet of paper measures 11 inches up and down in portrait mode. Click the **Portrait** button (⊡) in the bottom-left corner of the Print window to print in portrait mode. Landscape prints with the paper turned 90 degrees and the long edge of the page is oriented horizontally. Click the **Landscape** button (⊡) to print in landscape mode.

How can I maximize the size of my image on the printed page?

In the Print window, you can select the **Scale to Fit Media** option (■ changes to ☑) to scale the image to the maximum size for the current print settings.

Print Multiple Photos

Photoshop Elements makes it easy to print more than one photo from your photo catalog. You can choose from a variety of standard photo sizes and print each photo multiple times.

Print Multiple Photos

① In the Organizer, **Ctrl** -click to select the photos you want to print.

Note: *For details about using the Organizer, see Chapter 3.*

If none are selected, Elements includes all the photos currently displayed.

② Click **File**.

③ Click **Print**.

The Print Photos dialog box appears with the selected photos in the left column.

④ Click here and select your printer.

● You can click the **Show Printer Preferences** button (⊞) to select preferences specific to your printer.

⑤ Click here and select **Individual Prints**.

6 Click here and select a print size.

Elements displays a preview of the photos to be printed, on multiple pages if necessary.

● Click here to advance to the next page.

● Click here to go back to the previous page.

7 Type a number here to specify how many times each photo is to be printed.

● You can select the option to print one photo per page (■ changes to ✓).

8 Click **Print**.

Elements prints the photos.

TIP

How do I print multiple photos from the Editor?

1 Open the photos you want to print in the Editor.

2 Click **File**.

3 Click **Print Multiple Photos**.

Elements switches to the Organizer and opens the Print Photos dialog box.

4 Select options to print your photos.

Print a Picture Package

You can automatically create a one-page layout with one or more photos at various sizes to create a picture package. You may find this useful when you want to print pictures as gifts for friends or family.

1 In the Organizer, **Ctrl**-click to select the photos you want to display in your picture package.

Note: For details about using the Organizer, see Chapter 3.

If none are selected, Elements includes all the photos currently displayed.

2 Click **File**.

3 Click **Print**.

The Print Photos dialog box appears with the selected photos in the left column.

4 Click here and select your printer.

● You can click the **Show Printer Preferences** button (▦) to select preferences specific to your printer.

5 Click here and select **Picture Package**.

6 Click here and select a layout.

Elements automatically adds your photos to the layout.

To replace a photo, click and drag a photo from the left column to the layout.

● You can click here to add a custom frame to your photos in the picture package.

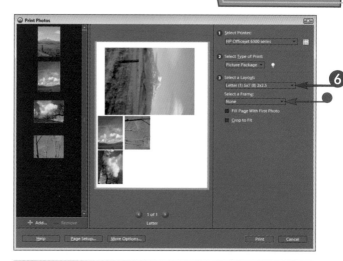

7 Click **Print**.

Elements prints your picture package.

How do I create a separate picture package layout for each selected photo?

1 When selecting your picture package options, click to select **Fill Page With First Photo** (☐ changes to ✓).

● Elements fills the layout with the first photo.

If you selected multiple photos, Elements places the other photos on their own separate pages.

● Click here to view the pages that follow.

● Click here to go back to previous pages.

Photoshop Elements can automatically create a digital version of a photographer's contact sheet, which consists of miniature versions of photos. Contact sheets are useful for keeping a hard-copy record of your digital images.

Print a Contact Sheet

① In the Organizer, **Ctrl**-click to select the photos you want to include on your contact sheet.

Note: For details about using the Organizer, see Chapter 3.

If none are selected, Elements includes all the photos currently displayed.

② Click **File**.

③ Click **Print**.

The Print Photos dialog box appears with the selected photos in the left column.

④ Click here and select your printer.

● You can click the **Preferences** button (⊞) to select preferences specific to your printer.

⑤ Click here and select **Contact Sheet**.

6 Type a number between 1 and 9 to specify the number of columns to include in the contact sheet.

Elements displays a preview of the contact sheet.

● You can click options to add text below the photos on the contact sheet.

If your selected photos do not fit on a single page, Elements creates multiple pages.

● Click here to advance to the next page.

● Click here to go back to the previous page.

7 Click **Print**.

Elements prints the contact sheet.

How do I print labels with my photos on them?

In the Print Photos dialog box, you can select **Labels** from the Type of Print menu to print labels. You can select from a variety of standard label layouts.

How do I make the photos larger or smaller on my contact sheet?

The size of the miniature photos on the contact sheet depends on the number of columns you select. To print bigger photos, select a smaller number of columns. To print smaller photos, select a larger number of columns. Choosing a portrait or landscape orientation for your printout can also affect the size of the photos on your contact sheet.

Export
Photos

You can export the photos in the Organizer to a folder. Elements lets you export your photos in a variety of file formats.

Export Photos

① Select the photos you want to export in the Organizer.

Note: For details about using the Organizer, see Chapter 3.

② Click **File**.

③ Click **Export**.

④ Click **As New Files**.

The Export New Files dialog box appears with the selected photos listed.

⑤ Click to select a file type (● changes to ○).

● Some file types allow you to specify a size or quality.

⑥ Click **Browse** to select a destination folder for the images.

⑦ To select more images to export, click **Add**.

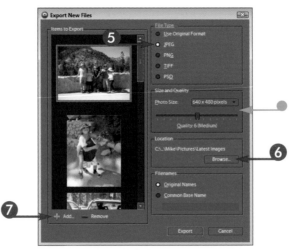

The Add Photos dialog box appears.

8 Click to select the photos you want to add
(■ changes to ✓).

9 Click **Done**.

Elements adds the photos.

● To remove a photo from the export list,
click the photo and then click **Remove**.

10 Click **Export**.

Elements exports your images.

TIP

How do I customize the names of my exported images?
You can customize the file names of your exported images in the
Export New Files dialog box:

1 Click to select **Common Base Name** (● changes to ○).

2 Specify a base name for your photo file names.

3 Click **Export**.

Elements exports your images.

Elements appends a hyphen and number to your base name to create
each file name.

You can back up your collection of digital photos using the Organizer's backup tool. This feature walks you through the steps for backing up your photo files to a CD, DVD, or other storage device.

Back Up Photos

① In the Organizer, open the catalog you want to back up.

Note: *For details about using the Organizer, see Chapter 3. For more about catalogs, see Chapter 3.*

② Click **File**.

③ Click **Backup Catalog to CD, DVD, or Hard Drive**.

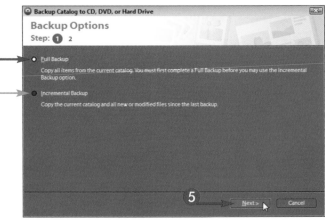

Elements may display a dialog box warning about missing files. If this happens, click **Reconnect** to perform a check.

The Backup Catalog to CD, DVD, or Hard Drive window opens.

④ Click to select the **Full Backup** option (● changes to ○).

● For subsequent backups, you can select the **Incremental Backup** option.

⑤ Click **Next**.

6 Click the drive to which you want to copy the backup files.

● You can type a name for the backup in this text box.

● Depending on your backup drive selection, the wizard displays an estimated file size and creation time.

7 Click **Done**.

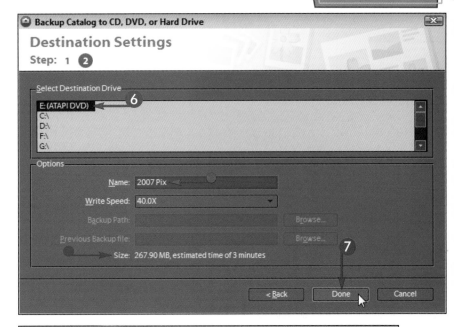

Photoshop Elements backs up your photos.

A prompt box alerts you when the procedure is complete.

You may have the option of verifying your backup when the backup is finished, depending on the media you used.

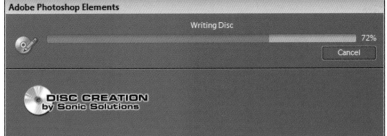

The Organizer prompts me to find missing files before backing up my photos. What do I do?

If any of the catalog photos no longer contain valid links to their original files, the backup tool displays a prompt box asking you to reconnect any missing files. A file can appear to be missing if you move it after adding the photo to the Organizer or if you rename the file outside of the Organizer. You can click **Reconnect** to allow Elements to look for the missing links and then continue with the backup.

How do I restore my backed-up files?

You can click **File** and then **Restore Catalog from CD, DVD, or Hard Drive** to restore backups of your photos onto your computer. The Restore dialog box offers options for restoring backed-up photos and catalogs to their original location or to a new location of your choosing.

Index

Index

Index

Index

Index

LP 513   163
LP 513   163

ANDERSON NONFICTION
25855339
006.686 Wooldridge, Mike
Wooldridge, Mike.
Photoshop Elements 6 / by Mike
Wooldridge and Linda Wooldridge.

NO LONGER PROPERTY OF
ANDERSON COUNTY LIBRARY

Anderson County Library
300 North McDuffie Street
Anderson, South Carolina 29621
(864) 260-4500

Belton, Honea Path, Iva,
Lander Regional, Pendleton,
Piedmont, Powdersville,
Westside, Bookmobile